Mexico

Mexico

BY R. CONRAD STEIN

Enchantment of the World
Second Series

Children's Press®

A Division of Grolier Publishing

NEW YORK   LONDON   HONG KONG   SYDNEY
DANBURY, CONNECTICUT

Consultant: James Cockcroft, Professor, Ramapo College of New Jersey

Please note: All statistics are as up-to-date as possible at the time of publication.

Visit Children's Press on the Internet: http://publishing.grolier.com

Book Production by Editorial Directions, Inc.
Book Design by Ox and Company

Library of Congress Cataloging-in-Publication Data

Stein, R. Conrad.
      Mexico / R. Conrad Stein.
      p. cm. — (Enchantment of the world. Second series)
      Includes bibliographical references and index.
      ISBN 0-516-20650-8
      1. Mexico—Juvenile literature. I. Title. II. Series.
      F1208.5.S73 1998
      972—dc21   97-40708
                                                            CIP
                                                            AC

To all my friends in
the town of San Miguel de Allende,
where I spent some of the
most rewarding years of my life

Contents

CHAPTER

 ONE Our Lady of Guadalupe 8

 TWO An Exciting Land 14

 THREE The Mexican Wilderness 24

 FOUR A Dramatic Past 30

 FIVE The Government of Mexico 46

 SIX The Economy 58

 SEVEN A Look at the People 72

 EIGHT A People of Faith 86

 NINE Mexicans at Ease 96

TEN Life in Mexico 110

Cover photo:
Folk dancer

Sierra Madre
mountain range

Timeline.....................128

Fast Facts....................130

To Find Out More...........134

Index.......................136

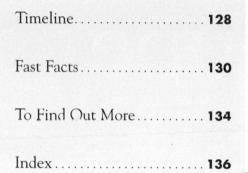

Iguana

Our Lady of Guadalupe

All Mexicans grow up hearing a very special story. The story takes place in 1531, just ten years after Spanish soldiers conquered the mighty Aztec nation of central Mexico.

On a bright December morning, a farmer named Juan Diego walked up a hill in the countryside near Mexico City. Juan was born an Aztec Indian and had grown up worshiping Aztec gods. Only recently had he become a Roman Catholic, adopting the religion brought to Mexico by the Spaniards. Near the hilltop, Juan heard the soft voice of a woman calling his name. Then he saw her. Radiant white light seemed to flow from her and arch upward toward the heavens. She told Juan Diego she wanted a church built on this hilltop.

"But . . . who are you?" Juan asked.

"I am the mother of all who live on this land," the woman said.

Juan Diego raced to Mexico City to tell the Catholic bishop what he saw. Bishop Zumárraga wanted to believe the woman was a messenger from God. Zumárraga was a Spaniard, and he was alarmed because his

A statue of Our Lady of Guadalupe in a Mexican graveyard

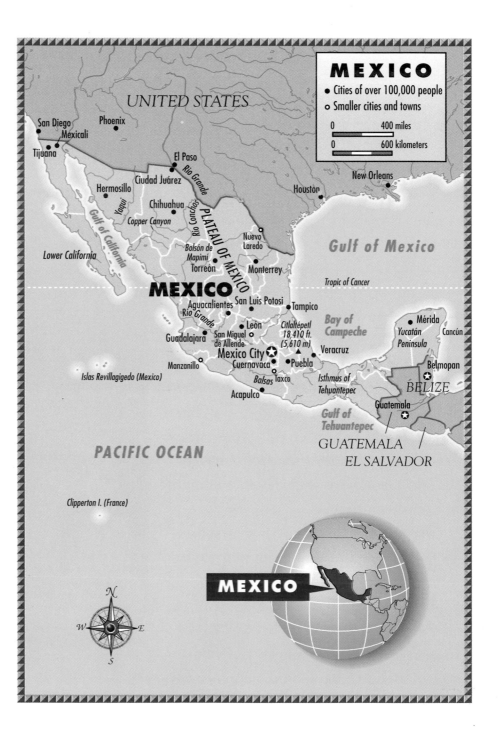

MEXICO

- Cities of over 100,000 people
- Smaller cities and towns

| 0 | 400 miles |
| 0 | 600 kilometers |

UNITED STATES

San Diego
Phoenix
Mexicali
Tijuana
El Paso
Río Grande
Ciudad Juárez
Houston
New Orleans
Hermosillo
Yaqui
Chihuahua
Copper Canyon
PLATEAU OF MEXICO
Río Conchos
Nuevo Laredo
Gulf of Mexico
Lower California
Bolsón de Mapimí
Torreón
Monterrey
Gulf of California
MEXICO
Tropic of Cancer
Aguacalientes
San Luis Potosí
Tampico
Bay of Campeche
Mérida
Río Grande
León
Yucatán Peninsula
Cancún
Guadalajara
San Miguel de Allende
Citlaltépetl 18,410 ft. (5,610 m)
Veracruz
Mexico City
Manzanillo
Cuernavaca
Puebla
Islas Revillagigedo (Mexico)
Balsas
Taxco
Isthmus of Tehuantepec
Belmopan
BELIZE
Acapulco
Gulf of Tehuantepec
Guatemala
PACIFIC OCEAN
GUATEMALA
EL SALVADOR

Clipperton I. (France)

N
W E
S

MEXICO

Geopolitical map
of Mexico

countrymen were enslaving the Aztecs and other Indian peoples. If an angel had indeed appeared to an impoverished Indian such as Juan, then perhaps he could convince his fellow-Spaniards that God looked upon the Indian people with favor. But the bishop needed evidence, some token of Juan's meeting.

Juan returned to the hill. Again he saw the beautiful woman. This time, the woman led him to the top of the hill where a lovely rosebush grew among the weeds and cactus plants. Juan was astonished. Roses had never grown on this spot before. He picked some of the flowers and tucked them under his straw vest, called a *tilma*. He then ran back to Mexico City.

Bishop Zumárraga was disappointed. A few roses growing on a hilltop were no proof that the woman was sent from heaven. Then Juan Diego opened his tilma to reveal the flowers, and the roses fell to the floor. The bishop stared, entranced, not at the roses, but at Juan's tilma. There, painted on the inside of the straw vest, was a wonderful portrait of a dark-skinned woman with a warm smile. No one—neither the bishop nor Juan Diego—was able to explain how the painting got there.

The tilma that bears the glorious painting hangs today in a golden frame above the altar in the Basilica of Guadalupe. This church stands on the hilltop where Juan had his vision. Catholic authorities regard the painting as a miracle and the woman is now called the Virgin of Guadalupe. The bishop said the picture was created by divine forces in hopes of

Souvenirs for sale outside the Basilica of Guadalupe

Opposite: **A statue stands at the site where Juan Diego is said to have seen the Virgin of Guadalupe.**

proving to Spaniards that the Indians too were children of God. Yet many historians believe the whole affair was a hoax. They claim that Bishop Zumárraga had a professional artist paint the picture. Art experts, however, point out that no painter in Mexico at that time was capable of creating such a fine portrait. Debate about the painting has never been resolved.

Still, most Mexicans believe the Juan Diego story was indeed a miracle. To millions of Mexicans, the Virgin of Guadalupe is a close friend, almost a family member. A painting of her is seen in practically every home. Bus drivers keep a tiny statue of the Virgin of Guadalupe near their rearview mirrors. In little grocery stores, her image stands on the highest shelves. And pilots for Mexicana Airlines have her statue somewhere in their cockpits.

Why is the Virgin of Guadalupe so honored in Mexico? Certainly one reason is because she is dark-skinned, unlike most other Catholic saints. Being dark, she was readily worshiped by the Indians and by the *mestizos*—a group of people that resulted from the intermarriage of Europeans and Indians.

Today, the Virgin of Guadalupe serves to unify Mexicans. Mexico is a society in which wide gaps exist between the rich and the poor. Yet nearly all Mexicans—rich or poor, light- or dark-skinned, powerful or powerless—praise Guadalupe and her miracle. She is Mexico's special saint, not to be shared with others. And Mexicans proudly speak of her as *our* Virgin of Guadalupe.

An Exciting Land

The Spanish conquerors of Mexico were led by a bold adventurer named Hernando Cortés. After the conquest, Cortés returned to Spain and the Spanish king asked him to describe the new lands. Cortés stammered, pointed upward, and drew wide circles with his hands. The king shifted impatiently on his throne. Finally, according to legend, Cortés grabbed a piece of paper. He crumpled the paper into a ball and presented it to the king. "There, your Majesty. Mexico looks like this."

Iɴ Mᴇxɪᴄᴏ, ᴊᴀɢɢᴇᴅ ᴍᴏᴜɴᴛᴀɪɴ ᴘᴇᴀᴋꜱ rise above the clouds and seem to kiss the sky. Cortés described the rugged landscape the best way he could.

Two gigantic mountain ranges— the Sierra Madre Oriental (East) and the Sierra Madre Occidental (West)—run the length of Mexico. One Mexican writer likened the two mountain chains to the braids of a

Mexico is known for its dramatic mountain ranges.

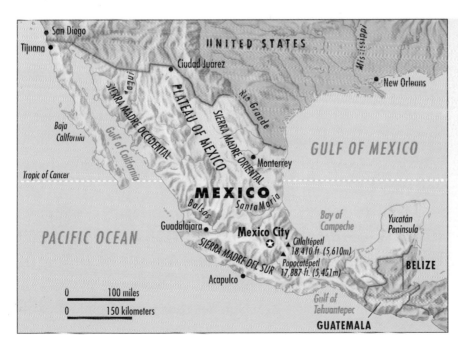

Geographical Features

Area: 756,066 square miles (1,958,201 sq km)

Highest Elevation: Citlaltépetl (also called Orizaba), 18,410 feet (5,610 m)

Lowest Elevation: Mexicali Valley, 33 feet (10 m) below sea level

Longest River: Lerma River, 350 miles (563 km)

Largest City: Mexico City

Average Annual Precipitation: Mexico City, 30 inches (76 cm) Monterrey, 23 inches (58 cm)

The Plateau of Mexico, the Nation's Heartland

Mexico's richest farmland and its largest cities all lie on this central plateau. Through most of its history, the majority of the nation's people have lived on the Plateau of Mexico. The five most populous cities, all of which are on the central plateau, are:

Mexico City	9,815,795
Guadalajara	
(pictured at left)	1,650,042
Netzahualcóyotl	1,255,456
Monterrey	1,068,996
Puebla	1,007,170

young girl draped across each side of the country. A central plateau, called the Plateau of Mexico, lies between the two ranges. Normally, a plateau is an elevated, flat expanse of land, but few places are flat in Mexico. The Plateau of Mexico has steep hills, towering mountains, and cone-shaped volcanoes.

Mexico's two mountain ranges flow gracefully down to the seacoasts. The Pacific coast, and more than 2,000 miles (3,200 km) of seashore, lies to the west. The Atlantic Ocean and the Gulf of Mexico spread to the east. This wealth of coastline includes many of the sunny beaches that give Mexico its well-deserved reputation as a vacationers' paradise.

In the south, the Yucatán Peninsula juts into the Atlantic. In the Yucatán region and much of southern Mexico, rain forests and grassy plains stretch across the land.

The Mexican beaches beckon tourists and fun lovers from many countries.

Mexico's Geography

A glance at a map shows that Mexico is a long narrow country that tapers as it runs south. A drive along its west coast, from the United States border in the north to Guatemala in the south, is almost as long as driving across the United States. In area, Mexico covers 756,066 square miles (1,958,201 sq km). This makes Mexico the fifth-largest country in the Americas, after Canada, the United States, Brazil, and Argentina.

A Gentle Climate

People from Canada and northern parts of the United States are astonished when they first visit Mexico. Business is conducted in the open air because most stores have no front wall.

Mexico's climate lends itself to outdoor activities.

Instead, they have overhead doors, like those on garages. At night, the storekeeper simply pulls the door down and locks it. Street vendors spread their goods on sidewalks, hoping to lure customers. This outdoor business continues even in the middle of January, when snow and ice have locked northern people inside their homes.

Mexico enjoys a gentle climate that encourages outdoor life. Even during winter months, people on the Plateau of Mexico wear light clothing, though they may have to wear a jacket at night. Summers are pleasant too. The Plateau of Mexico averages about 6,000 feet (1,800 m) above sea level. This mountain altitude discourages humidity, making air-conditioning in homes and stores unnecessary.

World-Famous Beach Resorts

Sun-worshipers and water-lovers from around the world flock to the hot lands for vacations. The endless silvery beaches are often seen on postcards. The city of Acapulco (left), on the Pacific Coast, has drawn visitors since the 1940s. The most popular tourist spot in recent years is Cancún, on the Gulf of Mexico.

In terms of climate, temperature changes in Mexico are vertical rather than horizontal. The temperatures do not necessarily get warmer as one goes south, but heat and humidity increase as one descends from the Plateau of Mexico to the seacoast. Sea-level country is called the *tierra caliente*, the hot land. People in the hot land must learn to live with a broiling sun and sultry humidity.

There is a flaw in Mexico's gentle climate, however—a chronic lack of rain. Over the Plateau of Mexico, the country's best farmland, the rainy season starts in May and lasts until October. If rain does not fall during those months, the farmers despair. Sometimes the entire population of a farming village will go to the fields and pray for the rains to begin. Some farm families hold the statue of a saint face-up to the heavens and beg the saint to send rain. Older farmers might silently pray to Tláloc, the ancient Aztec rain god.

MUSEO NACIONAL DE ANTROPOLOGIA

Tláloc, Still a Powerful Deity

More than 500 years ago, the Aztecs regarded Tláloc as the giver or withholder of rain. Thus Tláloc was a powerful deity in this rain-starved land. Dutifully the Aztecs carved stone statues of Tláloc and worshiped the figures. In 1964, workers removed a centuries-old sixty-ton statue of Tláloc from a rural village and set it up at the entrance of the new Museum of Anthropology in Mexico City. Villagers had warned that the move would make Tláloc angry and, just days after the statue was put in place, Mexico City was struck with a devastating rainstorm. It was the worst off-season storm in memory, and it caused severe flooding.

Risky Grounds

September 19, 1985, began like any other day in Mexico City. The sun rose. The morning traffic jam began. Then, just after 7 A.M., high-rise buildings suddenly swayed like palm trees bending in the wind. Windows shattered and glass rained down on the sidewalks.

At once, Mexico City residents understood. "*Terremoto!*" shouted people on the sidewalks. "Earthquake!"

Floors in downtown buildings collapsed on top of each other. A man on the twelfth floor of an apartment building said he felt a hollow sensation in his stomach, as if he were in an elevator plunging downward. Buildings that were ten stories high compacted to four stories in a matter of minutes. Thousands of people were buried under tons of debris.

Opposite: **Mexico City is a busy modern city.**

The 1985 earthquake lasted only a few seconds but it was the worst natural disaster to strike Mexico in modern times. The quake struck with an energy equal to 1,000 atomic bombs. So violent was the tremor that it shook buildings 600 miles (960 km) away in Texas. The government later announced that up to 10,000 people died, but many experts claim the number of deaths was twice that high. And at least 100,000 people were made homeless. To this day, survivors have nightmares about the morning the great city was flattened, as if struck by the hand of an angry god. In the days after the earthquake, Mexico City residents worked heroically to rescue men and women trapped under collapsed buildings.

Mexico is even more earthquake-prone than California. A particularly hazardous region lies south of Mexico City, where the nation's two major mountain ranges come together. Earthquakes in this area have terrorized Mexicans for hundreds of years.

Land of Volcanoes

Mexico has about 3,000 volcanoes, some of which are active and spew out smoke. Pictured above is the south face of Popocatépetl. It rises 17,887 feet (5,451 m) above the Mexican Central Plateau. New volcanoes can appear at any time. One volcano burst out of the ground some 250 miles (402 km) southwest of Mexico City in 1943. It grew so rapidly that hundreds of farm families living nearby had to flee for their lives. In just two months, the volcano had become a cone-shaped mountain standing 1,000 feet (304 m) over what was once a cornfield.

An earthquake devastated Mexico City in 1985.

The people of Mexico City cleaned up their streets and buried their dead after the 1985 earthquake. They went on with their lives, trying not to wonder when the next disaster would visit their city. But all Mexicans know that much of their country rests on unstable ground. "We'll suffer more great quakes," said Jorge Prince of the Mexican Society for Earthquake Engineering. "They may be even more destructive."

Despite drought, volcanoes, and earthquakes, Mexico is an uncommonly beautiful land. Anyone who has been there always longs to go back and experience again the thrilling vistas of its mountains and seacoasts.

The Pacific Ring of Fire

Volcanoes, ring of fire
Tectonic plates

The Mexican Wilderness

Early in the twentieth century, jaguars stalked the jungles of the Yucatán Peninsula and mountain lions roamed the Sierra Madre ranges. Those animals are still found in the Mexican wilds, but in vastly reduced numbers. Today, highways have penetrated nearly every corner of the nation. These roads bring in hunters who shoot game animals and farmers who clear forests to plant their crops.

The railroad leading into Copper Canyon

Yет Mexico's western Sierra Madre mountain range contains one sprawling land region that is simply too remote and too rugged for highway construction. South of the city of Chihuahua lies the Copper Canyon, a breathtaking gorge so deep that four Grand Canyons could fit inside it. You can visit the Copper Canyon by a railroad that took ninety years to build.

A jaguar in the Mexican wilderness

The Maya and the Cult of the Jaguar

The Maya, who once lived in the Yucatán region, were perhaps the most brilliant people of ancient Mexico. Their astronomers plotted the passage of stars and planets with astonishing precision. The Maya worshiped the jaguar, a creature of the Yucatán rain forests. The jaguar god was thought to regulate the underworld, where people went after death. During religious festivals, Mayan priests wore colorful jaguar masks and chanted special prayers.

Time stands still in the canyon. Deer, bear, and mountain lions roam free along the streams and on the patches of pine forests. The canyon is home to about 60,000 Tarahumara Indians, who live mainly by farming and hunting. The Copper Canyon is a spectacular reminder of wilderness Mexico in a bygone age.

Nature's Gifts to the Mountain Regions

The plants and animals of Mexico's mountains differ sharply from those found on the seacoasts. The mountain environment, with little rainfall and few cool nights, has nurtured a fantastic variety of plant and animal life.

A hiker in the mountains might get lucky and see a few of Mexico's large wild animals such as deer, bear, bobcats, and coyotes. But wildlife seekers in the mountains should keep their eyes on the ground and the sky. Vultures, some with 30-inch (76-cm) wingspans, fly above. They wheel around in graceful circles searching for an animal carcass to feast on. Snakes, rodents, and scurrying lizards are found at the hiker's feet. The rocky landscape of the mountains is alive with wild creatures.

The Plateau of Mexico has few trees but it is home to a wild assortment of cacti. Cactus plants store water in their stems, allowing them to live in an almost rainless climate. Almost 1,000 different kinds of cacti grow in Mexico, many in the mountainous regions. The saguaro, or giant cactus, grows so high that it looks like a tree. Some saguaros reach a height of 50 feet (15 m). The prickly pear cactus, which rises only knee high to the average person, is a great help to farmers. They use the sharp-quilled cactus like barbed wire, planting the cacti in squares to create pens for their cattle.

Mexicans use cactus plants in many ingenious ways. A flat-leaved cactus called nopal is stripped of its quills, cut into

Both the vulture and the cactus are native to Mexico.

Mangoes are among the exotic fruit that grows in Mexico.

tiny pieces, and fried in oil. Fried nopal with scrambled eggs is often served for breakfast. A refreshing cactus fruit called tuna tastes something like watermelon. The reddish tuna is covered with a fine coat of needlelike quills that can be peeled away only by experienced hands. Pulp from the agave cactus is used to make the fiery alcoholic drink known as tequila.

Wilderness in the Lowlands

Mexico is a land of contrasts. The great plateau hosts sprawling deserts, while the lowlands to the south and west are swampy. Exotic fruits such as mango and papaya grow in the wetlands. These fruits, along with bananas, oranges, and grapefruits, crowd stalls in southern markets. The fruits cost very little compared to similar produce sold in the United States. After heavy rains, the southern wetlands are ablaze with flowers—orchids, dahlias, and bougainvillea. Groves of coconut palms stand along the beaches.

The Joy of Chiclets

Sit in a city park for more than ten minutes and you are sure to be approached by a tiny child saying "Chiclets, chiclets! Want to buy chiclets?" The child will then hold up a package of chewing gum. The gum is the famous chicle, which has been enjoyed in Mexico for ages. Chiclets are sometimes used as money. A shopkeeper who has no change will give you packages of chiclets in place of coins. Chiclets are made from the pulp of the sapodilla tree, which grows in the southern wetlands.

Take a walk in the wetlands, and you will hear a haunting chorus of birdcalls. Herons, ducks, and geese fly in the lagoons. Flocks of pink flamingos feed in the swamps of the Yucatán. The south has the country's richest variety of animal life too. The speckled ocelot, which looks like a large cat, still stalks the southern forests. Spider monkeys swing along trees in the Mexican tropics. Some spider monkeys are also kept as pets, and some iguanas. The iguana is a large green lizard with a comblike row of scales running down its back. Dangerous animals such as alligators and poisonous snakes are also found in the tropics. No one makes pets out of these creatures.

The iguana is sometimes kept as a pet.

A Dramatic Past

More than 10,000 years ago, bands of hunters migrated from the north to settle in Mexico. Fossil evidence suggests that early settlers on the Plateau of Mexico hunted giant mammoths. Around 7000 B.C., the hunters learned how to cultivate corn. Farming gave the people stability and allowed them to develop advanced civilizations.

A carved stone monument from the Olmec

I N ABOUT 1200 B.C., A PEOPLE CALLED THE OLMEC built farming communities near the Gulf of Mexico. Their most lasting monuments are huge stone heads up to 10-feet (3-m) tall weighing 40 tons. Their faces have a curiously African look. Some historians suggest there was contact between the Olmec and the African people in ancient times.

Sometime about 200 B.C. a mysterious civilization built a great city about 35 miles (56 km) north of present-day Mexico City. At its most successful point, the ancient city held as many as 200,000 people. It was dominated by two massive pyramids that are today called the Pyramid of the Sun and the Pyramid of the Moon. For unknown reasons, that great city was abandoned and destroyed around A.D. 600–700. Today, its ruins attract thousands of visitors. More than 500 years ago, the Aztecs also held these ruins in awe. The Aztecs named the ghost city *Teotihuacán* (the place where gods are born).

The Pyramid of the Sun in Teotihuacán

The Mayan civilization reached its peak from A.D. 200 to 800. The Maya built vast cities in southern Mexico and

Opposite: **Mayan ruins in the Yucatán**

A wall painting depicting corn and the Aztec god of water

Central America. They were a gifted people whose scholars were devoted to the study of mathematics and astronomy. The calendar the Mayas devised was more accurate than any other in use at the time. The ancient Maya civilization collapsed suddenly and for unknown reasons. Today, Mayan people still live in southern Mexico. Some still speak their old language and observe the religious practices handed down by their illustrious ancestors.

The greatest builders in ancient Mexico were the Aztecs. About the year 1325, the Aztecs began constructing their masterpiece—the capital city of Tenochtitlán—on an island in the middle of a great, sparkling lake. The city had towering pyramids, ruler-straight streets, canals for boats carrying crops, and a marketplace where up to 60,000 people bought and sold goods.

An Aztec street in Tenochtitlán

The Aztecs were a warrior people. Their gods demanded the ultimate gift—the hearts of men and women. Aztec soldiers led long lines of victims to the tops of pyramids where

Corn, a Gift from a God

The Aztecs and other ancient Mexicans told a story about how people got corn. Long ago, according to the legend, only the ants harvested and ate corn. And the ants were determined to keep corn for themselves. They would not share the nourishing food with humans. But one day a god who loved humans turned himself into an ant and crawled into an anthill. Then the god carried out a kernel of corn and presented it to human beings.

For some time, the Aztecs believed that human sacrifices would strengthen the gods and result in good crops.

priests cut their hearts out and held them, still beating, in front of a god's statue. They believed the hearts were needed to make the gods bless the nation with rain, good crops, and victory in war. Other ancient peoples in Mexico and Europe also practiced bloody human sacrifice rituals, but few killed so many people in such brutal ways.

One Aztec god, however, condemned human sacrifice. His name was Quetzalcóatl. This gentle deity preferred gifts of flowers and butterflies to bloody human hearts. On wall paintings, Quetzalcóatl was pictured with white skin and a beard. He was in all respects a strange god in the Aztec pantheon.

The Spanish explorer Hernando Cortés (above) and the Aztec emperor Montezuma (below)

Spanish Rule

In 1519, an army of 500 Spanish soldiers splashed ashore at the beach near the present-day city of Veracruz. The Spaniards were an aggressive people who sought military conquest, gold, and converts for their Roman Catholic faith. Historians have summed up the Spaniards' mission in the Americas in three words: "god, gold, and glory." When the first soldiers asked the coastal people where they might find gold, the people pointed inland and said, "Mexico, Mexico." "Mexico" was the coastal people's word for the Aztec capital of Tenochtitlán.

The Spaniards were led by Hernando Cortés. As he marched inland, Cortés preached the Christian religion to the Indians he encountered and he also told them that human sacrifice was a sin. His actions alarmed Montezuma, the Aztec emperor. Cortés was a bearded white man who looked like the wall paintings of the god Quetzalcóatl. And like the ancient god, this stranger denounced human sacrifice. Was the foreigner a god, Montezuma wondered? What could Montezuma—a mere mortal—do when he was confronted by a god?

The Quetzalcóatl Coincidences

According to legend, Quetzalcóatl was driven out of Mexico by a rival god. He vowed to return in the year One Reed and reclaim the land. On the Aztec calendar, One Reed is 1519, the same year the Spaniards landed at Veracruz. This date is one of several strange coincidences that led many Aztecs to believe Cortés was a god.

When the Spaniards entered Tenochtitlán they were worshiped as deities, but the Aztecs soon learned these foreigners were men, not gods. A war broke out between the Aztecs and the Spaniards. Many neighboring Indian nations who had long hated the powerful Aztecs fought side by side with the Spaniards. In 1521, the Spaniards and their allies conquered the Aztecs. The victors established their own empire and called it New Spain.

A casualty of the war was the magnificent Aztec capital of Tenochtitlán. The great city was reduced to rubble during the fighting. The Spaniards immediately began building a new city over the wreckage of the old. Often they used bricks from Aztec pyramids to construct houses and churches. The new city—Mexico City— served as the capital of New Spain for the next 300 years.

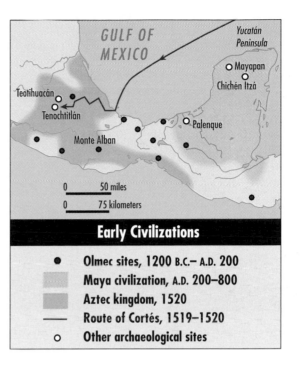

Early Civilizations

- ●   **Olmec sites, 1200 B.C.– A.D. 200**
-      **Maya civilization, A.D. 200–800**
-      **Aztec kingdom, 1520**
- —   **Route of Cortés, 1519–1520**
- ○   **Other archaeological sites**

The Spaniards destroyed Mexican idols when they conquered Tenochtitlán.

Spanish Strength

Spanish soldiers brought guns, horses, and iron swords to the battlefield. Never before had the Aztec army fought against such well-armed men. And the Spaniards had a hidden weapon. Unknowingly, the soldiers carried European diseases to the Americas. In the final battles, the Aztecs were so weakened by smallpox that many could hardly walk, much less fight.

Ghosts of Tenochtitlán

The ruins of old Tenochtitlán lie like coffins in a graveyard beneath the streets and buildings of Mexico City. But every now and then, those ancient coffins resurface. In the 1970s, construction workers came upon a vast temple complex buried below downtown Mexico City. The complex was carefully excavated and it is now preserved as an outdoor museum called *Templo Mayor* (Main Temple).

After the conquest, thousands of Spaniards immigrated to New Spain, bringing the Spanish language and the Christian religion with them. Indian people became eager converts to Christianity, especially after the picture of the Lady of Guadalupe miraculously appeared on Juan Diego's straw vest in 1531.

The Spaniards freely intermarried with the Aztecs and other Indians. As a result, three classes of people emerged in Mexican society: whites, Indians, and a new group—the mestizos. From the beginning, the whites held all the power. They allowed the mestizos meager privileges, but treated the Indians as a defeated people.

Modern-day Guanajuato, capital of the state of Guanajuato, in central Mexico

More than 12,000 churches were built during the era of New Spain. Handsome cities such as Guadalajara, Guanajuato, and Taxco came into being. Mexico City became the most impressive metropolis in the Americas. All the cities were graced with Spanish colonial architecture, a delicate blending of European styles and local materials. Indian artists created brilliant statues and wall paintings to adorn the churches. Spanish priests were astounded by their skills.

The Spaniards also found a fortune of untapped gold and silver beneath the ground in Mexico. Some 5,000 Spanish-run silver mines operated in New Spain. Indians, who were virtual slaves, worked the mines under brutal Spaniards. The treasures of gold and silver allowed Spain to build a mighty fleet of warships and thus become a major power in Europe.

From its beginnings, the government of New Spain was rigidly controlled by Spanish authorities far away across the

Imported Diseases, the Scourge of the Indians

By simply coming to the Americas, the Spaniards exposed the Indians to smallpox, measles, diphtheria, and many other sicknesses that Europeans had lived with for hundreds of years. The Europeans had built up enough immunity so that the diseases sickened them but no longer killed them in large numbers. However, the Indian people had no such immunity. Within thirty years of the Spaniards' arrival, the Indian population of central Mexico was cut in half by killer epidemics.

Atlantic Ocean. The Mexican people longed for self-government and freedom from Spain. After 300 years of Spanish rule, Mexicans began to whisper an exciting but dangerous word—*Independencia!* (Independence!)

Early on the morning of September 15, 1810, a priest named Miguel Hidalgo y Costilla rang a church bell as if to summon his parishioners to mass. But instead of celebrating mass, Father Hidalgo issued a call for revolution. It was the beginning of the Mexican War of Independence.

A New Nation

The War of Independence lasted for eleven years. Mexican patriots achieved independence from Spain, but the nation was sadly unprepared for self-government. A long and dismal period of political instability followed. Presidents were changed through army rebellions rather than by free elections.

Political confusion left Mexico vulnerable to its powerful neighbor—the United States. In the early 1800s, Mexico's northern border included what is today the southwestern United States: Texas, New Mexico, Arizona, California, and parts of Nevada, Utah, and Colorado. All those states were named by Spanish and Mexican pioneers who settled on the lands. Now the ever-expanding United States wanted those territories.

Texas began the road to war. For years, U.S. settlers had entered Texas with the approval of the Mexican

The fall of the Alamo

government. In 1836, the settlers declared Texas to be an independent nation. A terrible battle broke out at an old church called the Alamo in San Antonio, Texas. Mexican troops, led by General Santa Anna, crushed the revolt, slaughtering the Alamo defenders. Ten years later, the United States went to war under the battle cry, "Remember the Alamo!"

The Mexican-American War, fought from 1846 to 1848, was a disaster for Mexico. American troops occupied the sea-

Opposite: **A monument to Father Hidalgo stands in the town of Dolores Hidalgo.**

Mexican Independence Day

Father Hidalgo launched the War of Independence at the doorstep of his church in the town of Dolores (now called Dolores Hidalgo), about 150 miles (240 km) north of Mexico City. There he made a famous speech—the *"Grito de Dolores"* (Cry of Dolores)—that spurred the people to action. No one knows his exact words. Today, speakers reenact the Grito on the night of September 15 by shouting out *"Viva Hidalgo"* (Long Live Hidalgo!) "Viva independencia! Viva Mexico!" Crowds gather at town squares and repeat each chant: "Viva! Viva! Viva!" Finally fireworks explode, church bells ring, and bands play the Mexican National Anthem. The next day, September 16, is Mexican Independence Day. This joyous day is celebrated with parades and patriotic music in Mexico and by people of Mexican heritage who live in other countries.

Slavery and the Texans

Most of the Texan settlers came from the southern United States, where slavery was permitted and many Texans owned slaves. The slaves worked on Texas farms and cattle ranches. But Mexican law banned slavery so government authorities in Mexico City ordered the Texans to free their slaves. The Texans refused. Often U.S. history books hail the Texans and their fight for freedom against Mexico. Ironically, one of the freedoms the Texans fought for was their "freedom" to own slaves.

port of Veracruz and marched into Mexico City. As a result of the war, Mexico was forced to hand over its northern territories to the United States. To this day, many Mexicans ponder this incredible loss of land and feel bitter toward their mighty neighbor to the north.

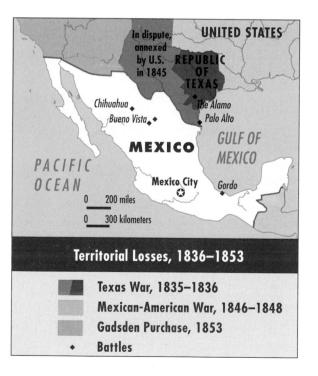

Territorial Losses, 1836–1853

- Texas War, 1835–1836
- Mexican-American War, 1846–1848
- Gadsden Purchase, 1853
- ◆ Battles

Confusion and civil war continued to plague Mexico after its defeat at the hands of the United States in 1848. In 1853, the United States purchased from Mexico a narrow strip of land called the Gadsden Purchase. From 1863 to 1867, French troops occupied Mexico. The French installed an archduke of Austria named Maximilian to rule the nation. Maximilian was finally overthrown and was executed by Mexico's legitimate president, Benito Juárez.

In 1876, the army General Porfirio Díaz took power in Mexico. Except for a brief period, he ruled for the next thirty

The Remarkable Benito Juárez

A full-blooded Zapotec Indian, Benito Juárez was born in severe poverty. Orphaned at the age of three, he worked as a houseboy, but managed to get an education. Juárez became president in 1858 while civil war raged in Mexico. As president, he promoted education and tried to reduce the power the Catholic Church held over the country. He died in office in 1872.

years. He was an iron-fisted leader whose policies brought an end to army rebellions and civil wars. Díaz tried to modernize Mexico by building railroads and encouraging the expansion of factories.

The Díaz government achieved progress, but the gap between rich and poor grew at an alarming rate. Land ownership became a burning issue. Before the Díaz era some 20 percent of the Mexican people owned at least a small plot of land; by 1910, only 2 percent were landowners. Meanwhile, a handful of wealthy families amassed huge plantations.

Modern Mexico, a Society Forged by Revolution

In late 1910, Mexico boiled over like a stew left too long on the fire. In the north, rebels waged war under a one-time cattle thief and bandit named Francisco "Pancho" Villa. In the south, the peasant general Emiliano Zapata led landless farmers on hit-and-run attacks against wealthy plantations. Aging President Porfirio Díaz was forced to leave Mexico. A democratic idealist named Francisco Madero became president but the mild-mannered Madero could not hold together a nation torn by war and hatred. Madero was executed by the pro-Díaz army general, Victoriano Huerta. With Huerta in power, the great Mexican Revolution erupted.

Pancho Villa

From 1910 to 1920, civil war swept across Mexico like a whirlwind. Rebels fought government forces, and rebel generals fought each other. Not even frontline troops knew what principles they were fighting for. When an American journalist asked a teenaged soldier from northern Mexico why he was fighting, the soldier said, "Why it is good—fighting—you don't have to work in the mines."

The Mexican Revolution was the bloodiest war ever fought in the Americas, surpassing even the slaughter of the American Civil War. At least 1 million and perhaps as many as 2 million Mexicans died in the fighting. In 1920, the war ended without a

Mexico's Presidents Since 1920

Alvaro Obregòn	1920–1924
Plutarco Elías Calles	1924–1928
Emilio Portes Gil	1928–1930
Pascual Ortiz Rubio	1930–1932
Abelardo L. Rodriguez	1932–1934
Lázaro Cárdenas	1934–1940
Manuel Avila Camacho	1940–1946
Miguel Alemán	1946–1952
Adolfo Ruiz Cortines	1952–1958
Adolfo López Mateos	1958–1964
Gustavo Díaz Ordaz	1964–1970
Luis Echeverría Álvarez	1970–1976
José López Portillo	1976–1982
Miguel de la Madrid	1982–1988
Carlos Salinas de Gortari	1988–1994
Ernesto Zedillo Ponce de Léon	1994–

Viva Zapata!

One hero, Emiliano Zapata, rose like a brilliant star from the bloodshed of the Mexican Revolution. Born in the southern state of Morelos, Zapata wanted no power for himself. Instead, he fought for the rights of landless farmers. "Land and liberty" was the battle cry of his followers. Zapata was ambushed and killed by dozens of riflemen in 1919, but many claim he defied death itself. For years, people in the south claimed they still saw Zapata riding at night on a gleaming white horse.

clear winner—the exhausted people simply could not fight any longer.

Despite the terrible bloodshed, Mexico emerged from the fighting more unified than ever before. Gone were the old class distinctions among whites, Indians, and mestizos. Now all were Mexicans. A new constitution, written in 1917, separated church and state and guaranteed the rights of workers. In the decades after the revolution, the nation enjoyed an artistic rebirth. Mexican painters became famous throughout the world.

During World War II (1939–1945), Mexico aided the United States by participating in the *Bracero* program (often

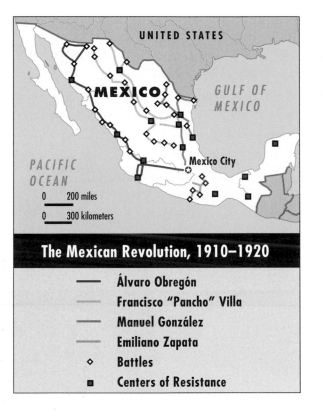

The Mexican Revolution, 1910–1920

— Álvaro Obregón
— Francisco "Pancho" Villa
— Manuel González
— Emiliano Zapata
◇ Battles
■ Centers of Resistance

translated as "helping hand"). The program allowed Mexican farmworkers to come north and help bring in harvests. Thousands of rural Mexicans got their first view of the United States while working as braceros.

After the war, Mexico enjoyed a period of prosperity and political peace. Certainly, many Mexicans lived in wretched poverty, but the public school system was now open to all and Mexico had a wealth of oil to export to other nations.

Then, in the late 1970s, a currency crisis brought devastating inflation to Mexico. Almost overnight the country's currency, the peso, plunged in value. Economists blamed the sudden devaluation on Mexico's huge foreign debt. The weakened peso wiped out the savings of the workers. At one time, a working family thought having 1,000 pesos in the bank was a comfortable hedge against sickness or job loss. By the mid-1980s, 1,000 pesos—the life savings for many families—was the price of a candy bar.

In the 1990s, the old scourge of political instability and armed rebellion emerged in Mexico once more. In the

southern state of Chiapas, landless farmers fought pitched battles with the Mexican army. One band of farmers marched under the banner of the revolutionary war hero Emiliano Zapata. Remembering his spirit, the farmers called themselves the "Zapatistas."

Rebels, known as "Zapatistas," hide their faces from photographers.

Opposite: **A worker in the Bracero program**

The Government of Mexico

Mexico is officially called *Estados Unidos Mexicanos* (United Mexican States). Like its neighbor to the north, Mexico is divided into states, each one with its own capital city and self-government responsibilities. Mexico has thirty-one states and one federal district. The federal district surrounds Mexico City, the nation's capital.

M EXICO IS A REPUBLIC—A NATION WITHOUT A KING OR queen. It is also a democracy. All citizens age eighteen or older may vote.

The federal government has great powers over the workings of the country. Through taxes, it raises and spends most of the nation's money. It can seize land and businesses in the name of the common good.

States have a governor and a legislature based on the federal system. Under special circumstances, the federal government can replace a state governor or suspend a state legislature. Towns are governed by a *presidente* (president) and a city council. A town or city can also be taken over by the federal government if federal authorities feel such action is necessary to keep the peace.

Opposite: **The National Palace in Mexico City**

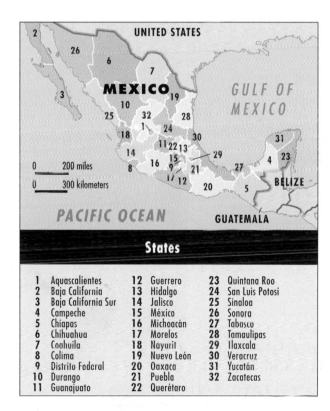

#	State	#	State	#	State
1	Aguascalientes	12	Guerrero	23	Quintana Roo
2	Baja California	13	Hidalgo	24	San Luis Potosi
3	Baja California Sur	14	Jalisco	25	Sinaloa
4	Campeche	15	México	26	Sonora
5	Chiapas	16	Michoacán	27	Tabasco
6	Chihuahua	17	Morelos	28	Tamaulipas
7	Coahuila	18	Nayarit	29	Tlaxcala
8	Colima	19	Nuevo León	30	Veracruz
9	Distrito Federal	20	Oaxaca	31	Yucatán
10	Durango	21	Puebla	32	Zacatecas
11	Guanajuato	22	Querétaro		

Ask Mexicans how they vote, and most will say, "With the Party." They are talking about the Party of Revolutionary Institutions (PRI)—the most powerful political organization in the country. Established in the late 1920s, the PRI claims to uphold the lofty goals of the Mexican Revolution. For years, it was the only political party that mattered in Mexico. Although lesser parties existed, the PRI won the presidency in every election. The PRI was, in effect, an arm of the government. Candidates for president were chosen in closed-door meetings by party leaders. Those candidates were then presented to the voters. Because the country was virtually under a one-party system, the PRI candidate always won.

The Mexican Coat of Arms

An eagle sitting on a cactus while eating a snake—this is the image in the center of the Mexican flag. The image is from the time the Aztecs were a wandering people seeking a homeland. According to legend, a god told the Aztecs to look for a place where they would see an eagle perched on a cactus while devouring a snake. On that site they should build the capital city of their new nation. Tradition says they found this magical spot in the year 1325. Immediately, the Aztecs began building the city of Tenochtitlán (Place of the Cactus). Tenochtitlán became Mexico City, and the mythical eagle is now on Mexico's coat of arms.

Workings of the Federal Government

The Constitution of 1917 spells out the rules for the federal government. Similar to the U.S. Constitution, the Mexican Constitution divides the nation's government into three branches—executive, legislative, and judicial.

The executive department is headed by the president. His or her job is to enforce the country's laws. The Constitution gives the president wide powers to make important appointments and to command the armed forces. The president is elected for one six-year term and cannot run for re-election. There is no vice president. The legislative branch appoints a replacement if the president cannot finish a term.

The legislative department consists of a sixty-four-member Senate (two senators from each state plus two from the federal district) and a 500-member Chamber of Deputies. Senators are elected to one six-year term. Deputies serve three-year terms; they can be reelected, but cannot serve two terms in a row. The legislature is a law-making body. Its members create new laws and rescind old ones.

The Judicial Department is made up of the court system. The nation's highest court, the Supreme Court of Justice, has twenty-one members, all of whom are appointed by the president.

Carlos Salinas de Gortari *(center)* **was backed by the PRI in the 1988 presidential election.**

Charges of Vote Fraud

In 1988, the PRI candidate, Carlos Salinas de Gortari, was elected president by a narrow margin. His main opponent was Cuauhtémoc Cárdenas of the Democratic Revolutionary Party (PRD). The son of a much-beloved former president, Cárdenas enjoyed great popular support.

Many Mexicans thought he would be the first president to break the PRI rule. When he lost, Cárdenas loyalists claimed PRI authorities, who oversaw the elections, cheated on the vote count. The charge of vote fraud sparked violent demonstrations and riots around the country.

Then, in the 1988 election, non-PRI candidates won almost half the seats in the Chamber of Deputies, and they almost gained the presidency. In 1989, the PRI lost a governorship for the first time. The sudden popularity of opposition parties, such as the PAN (National Action Party), shocked many political observers. Some feared the weakening of the PRI would undermine the Mexican government. Others, however, considered the emergence of rival parties to be a sign of political health in Mexico.

The "Little Bite"

Claudia is a seventeen-year-old who lives in the Yucatán city of Mérida. Like many teenagers, she wanted a driver's license, so she went to her township office to ask for the application papers. A man there told her to see a *licenciado* (legal aide). The licenciado said Claudia must pay him a fee for legal services. Also she had to give him money that he would pass on to a township clerk as a "tip." The clerk would the issue the driver's license application papers only after receiving the money. This tip, Claudia knew, was called a *mordida*, a "little bite."

Paying the little bite is an institution in Mexico. If a police officer stops a driver for speeding, the officer will often accept a mordida on the street instead of taking the driver to court. Workers for utility companies sometimes operate under the mordida system. If your telephone is out of service, a mordida to the service person will ensure your phone gets fixed much more quickly. In some towns, even the garbage collectors demand a mordida before they collect the garbage.

Luis Donaldo Colosio

Generally, the people collecting the mordidas do not think of themselves as dishonest. They would not dream of stealing money from another person or taking anything from anyone's house. Instead, they look upon mordidas as part of their pay, a harmless fee for services rendered.

The mordida system also enters high government circles. There the "little bite" can become a very big bite indeed. In the late 1980s a journalist wrote a report on Mexico City's chief of police. The chief lived in a suburban mansion with fifteen bedrooms, five swimming pools, and even a horseracing track on its grounds. The estate was worth $2.5 million. The chief's official salary was about $65 a month. Clearly, bribery and corruption paid for the chief's grand house.

Opposite: **The mansion belonging to the former Mexico City chief of police**

Lázaro Cárdenas (1895–1970), Beloved President of Mexico

Lázaro Cárdenas was president of Mexico from 1934 to 1940. As president, he listened to the problems of poor farmers. He often hiked or rode a burro to isolated farm communities that had no roads. He was revered for the attention he paid to impoverished people. Cárdenas was also popular because of his bold stand against the United States. In 1938 he seized the foreign oil firms operating in Mexico. Many of these oil companies were owned by U.S. interests. The oil-company owners denounced Cárdenas as a criminal, but Mexicans hailed him as a hero. In 1988, his son, Cuauhtémoc Cárdenas, was almost elected president. Then, in 1997, Cuauhtémoc Cárdenas was elected mayor of Mexico City. Many leaders urged him to run for president in the year 2000.

The most shocking example of corruption in high places came in 1993 when Luis Donaldo Colosio, the PRI candidate for president, was shot and killed while campaigning in Tijuana. Journalists claimed it was a political assassination, a charge initially denied by government officials. Investigations into the murder revealed that high-ranking politicians had secret bank accounts containing millions of dollars. The brother of Mexican President Carlos Salinas de Gortari was found to have a multimillion-dollar bank account in Switzerland. In 1997, Swiss authorities seized that money, charging it came from drug dealers.

Mexicans are outraged and disgusted at the corruption of their officials and political leaders. Meanwhile, on the streets, they pay the little bite to local police, and life goes on as always.

El Norte

Mexicans have a saying: "Poor Mexico; so far from God, so close to the United States." Mexico is a developing country where masses of people live in poverty. But the richest, most powerful country on earth lies across a very thin borderline. Nowhere else in the world does such a poor land touch borders with such a wealthy land, separated only by what amounts to a back fence.

The United States is called *El Norte* (The North) by the Mexican people. Millions dream of going to El Norte, working there, and getting a share of that land's riches. But they also fear the power of their neighbor. No one forgets the 1846–1848 war that cost Mexico almost half its territory. As recently as 1914, U.S. troops occupied the port city of Veracruz to prevent arms shipments from going to revolutionaries.

Today, Mexicans often charge that the United States tries to tell Mexicans how to govern themselves. Consider, for example, the problem of air pollution coming from Ciudad Juarez and spoiling the air above El Paso, Texas. El Paso lies just across the Rio Grande from Ciudad Juarez. When pollution worsens in the summer months, El Paso authorities suggest that people in Ciudad Juarez ought to burn less-polluting gasoline in their automobiles. The Mexicans claim that the gasoline sold in Mexico is their business and not the concern of anyone in El Norte.

The border between the United States and Mexico stretches about 2,000 miles (3,200 km). In the east (facing Texas and much of New Mexico), the border is well defined by the Rio Grande. To the west it is a land border, a line stretching all the way to the Pacific Ocean. There are many "soft spots" along this border—places where illegal immigrants or drug smugglers can cross undetected. The border area is also a distinct region in Mexico. At border cities such as Tijuana and Ciudad Juárez, children learn English by watching cartoons broadcast from the United States. Dollars are exchanged freely in the stores there along with pesos. Mexicans call the border region *La Frontera* (The Frontier).

Drug-smuggling across the border is an explosive problem facing the two countries. It is estimated that two-thirds of the illegal drugs entering the United States are brought in from Mexico. However, not all those drugs are manufactured in Mexico. Drug traffickers from other nations often bring their products into Mexico and then smuggle them across the border.

For years, the United States helped to fund a program within Mexico that detected drug smugglers. Then, in 1997, the Mexican army general who headed the anti-drug unit was arrested. The general was charged with taking payoff money from drug dealers. After the arrest the U.S. Congress wanted to cut off funds for the drug-fighting program. Mexican officials complained that the United States was once more bullying its smaller neighbor.

Close neighbors are bound to have some problems. Despite frequent squabbles, relations with the United States are good. Almost 14 million Mexican Americans live in the United States. More than neighbors, the two countries can be considered family members.

The Economy

The northern Mexico city of Monterrey has more than 500 major factories producing concrete, iron, steel, and clothing. For its size, Monterrey is the most industrialized city in Mexico. Yet take a walk in Monterrey and you'll see people selling newspapers, shining shoes, or peddling candy bars on the streets. Most of the people who work as street vendors would prefer a steady job in one of the city's factories. However, there simply are not enough jobs for the masses of workers.

MEXICO HAS A YOUNG POPULATION. More than half the nation's people are under twenty years of age. Every year, about a million young men and women reach working age and begin to look for jobs. But even in good times, job growth does not keep up with population growth. Young people find few opportunities. Estimates say that 30 percent of the country's workers need full-time jobs. True unemployment figures are difficult to compile because Mexicans are never idle. When they have no steady jobs, they work as street vendors, helpers on delivery trucks, or even as scavengers in garbage dumps. Because these casual workers have some means of earning money, the government does not consider them to be unemployed. Mexico has no welfare system that pays cash to the destitute. Instead everyone must find some way to earn a living. Surprisingly, only a small percentage become beggars or turn to crime.

Many Mexicans work as street vendors.

Opposite:
The city of Monterrey

Dangers of a Border Crossing

In February 1997, Martin Facio, an auto mechanic from Mexico City, attempted to sneak across the border. Near Tijuana, he faced high barbed-wire fences and many border patrols. So Facio crossed through a desert region some 50 miles (80 km) to the east. He walked across the border without being detected. But in the middle of the night, the temperature dropped to below freezing and the wind began to howl. Facio was pelted with rain and sleet. He did not know that fourteen other illegal immigrants had died of exposure in this area in the past month. Finally, he spotted a group of border agents and begged to be captured. Will he try to cross again? "Yes," said Facio. "But next time I'll wear a warm pair of gloves."

The Lure of the North

A semiskilled worker in a Monterrey factory earns the equivalent of about $6 a day. A few hundred miles to the north, in the United States, factories pay $6 an hour for the same work. It is no wonder that Mexicans long to go to El Norte to work.

Each year, the United States accepts more immigrants from Mexico than it does from any other country in the world. Still, the wait for legal admission can take many years. Desperate people feel they cannot wait. It is estimated that 1.75 million Mexicans live and work illegally in the United States.

A Mexican family crossing the Rio Grande into Brownsville, Texas

Most illegal workers are men who hold jobs, live frugally, and send money back to their families. They look upon the border as a revolving door. The illegals return to Mexico for holidays or when they are feeling terribly lonely for their families. After a brief visit, they go back again to *el otro lado* (the other side). They return by wading across the Rio Grande, by hiking at night through a lonely desert area, or by hiding in a boxcar or in the back of a truck. Every year, U.S. border patrol agents arrest about 1 million illegal immigrants. Those arrested are sent back to Mexico, where most try to cross again—through the revolving door.

Business owners in the United States know that Mexicans, whether they are legal or illegal immigrants, are hard workers. They are willing to take low-paying, menial jobs that are often shunned by U.S. citizens. Mexicans pick cotton under the hot Texas sun, they wash dishes in the steamy kitchens of restaurants, and many are skilled bricklayers, carpenters, or electricians. Whatever their jobs, Mexicans generally perform well and make few complaints. The illegals cannot complain to government authorities about poor working conditions. In the eyes of the government, the illegals are criminals and they have no protection under the law.

Jobs and Resources

In 1994, Canada, the United States, and Mexico signed the North American Free Trade Agreement (NAFTA). The agreement cut tariffs, allowing goods to pass more or less freely among the three countries. From the beginning, labor interests in the

United States opposed NAFTA. Labor unions argued that free trade would allow factory owners to buy parts and products made by low-paid Mexican workers. The owners could then fire higher-paid factory hands in the United States. Without a doubt, the passage of NAFTA has created thousands of new fac-

The Japanese company Sanyo has a factory in Tijuana

tory jobs in Mexico. How many jobs NAFTA has cost north of the border is still a matter of debate.

Even before the passage of NAFTA, huge factory complexes were built in Mexico along the U.S. border. The factories, called *maquiladores*, were established to take advantage of the lower wages paid in Mexico. Most of the maquiladores are owned by U.S. companies. Workers in the border plants manufacture car parts and assemble computers and television sets.

A farmer shares corn with a neighbor who has helped him plant his field.

The final products are often sold in the United States. By the mid-1990s, more than 2,000 maquiladores along the border employed about 500,000 Mexican workers.

Wages in Mexico remain low despite the sharp growth of factory jobs. Because so many people want full-time jobs, workers are easily replaced. A factory owner need not pay a man or woman more than $6 a day when there are a dozen people waiting in line outside, willing to work for $5.

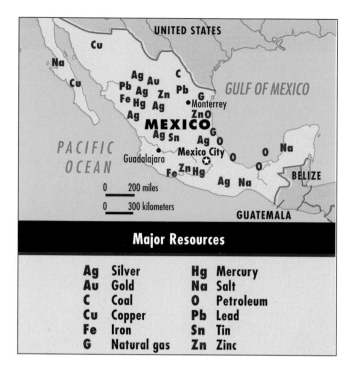

Major Resources

Ag	Silver	Hg	Mercury
Au	Gold	Na	Salt
C	Coal	O	Petroleum
Cu	Copper	Pb	Lead
Fe	Iron	Sn	Tin
G	Natural gas	Zn	Zinc

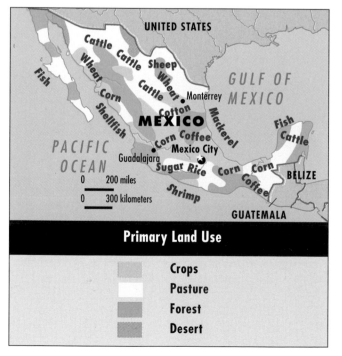

Primary Land Use

- Crops
- Pasture
- Forest
- Desert

About 50 percent of Mexican workers are employed in the service industries. Service workers provide a service rather than produce a product. Schoolteachers, store clerks, and accountants at a bank are all service workers. Tourism creates service jobs in hotels and restaurants. Mexico has a pleasant climate, friendly people, and sparkling beaches. For these reasons, more than 6 million visitors arrive each year. Tourism is the country's largest single source of employment.

Only 12 percent of Mexico's total land area is used for farming. Rocky soil and poor rainfall make most of the land unsuitable for crops. The best farmland is found in the southern half of the Plateau of Mexico. In the southern lowlands, rain is plentiful, but inadequate drainage turns the land into soggy marshes. Corn, the major crop throughout the country, is used to make tortillas, the common bread of Mexico. Other important crops include bananas, cotton, lemons, mangoes, and oranges.

What Mexico Grows, Makes, and Mines

Agriculture (1995)

Sugarcane	42,562,000 metric tons
Corn	16,187,000 metric tons
Sorghum	4,169,000 metric tons

Manufacturing (1993) *(in Mexican pesos)*

Machinery and equipment	82,169,495,000
Food, beverages, & tobacco products	64,399,498,000
Chemical products	50,455,651,000

Mining (1993) *(in Mexican pesos)*

Copper	2,236,437,000
Silver	1,339,057,000
Zinc	1,321,759,000

Oil is a billion-dollar industry, second only to manufacturing. Mexico is Latin America's leading oil producer and ranks sixth in the world in terms of oil reserves still in the ground. But oil production, unlike manufacturing, does not generate large numbers of jobs. Also, oil is subject to sharp price changes on the world market. Through most of the 1980s and 1990s the worldwide price of oil was low.

Mexico ranks as the world's leading silver producer. About one-sixth of the world's annual production of silver comes from Mexico. Copper, gold, lead, salt, and zinc are also taken from Mexico's mines.

Rich and Poor—A Widening Gap

A lush green park called the Alameda spreads out in the heart of Mexico City. Wealthy bankers and politicians enjoy sitting on park benches and reading newspapers there. Joel Flores Gonzales is also sitting in the park. He is a shoe-shine man who

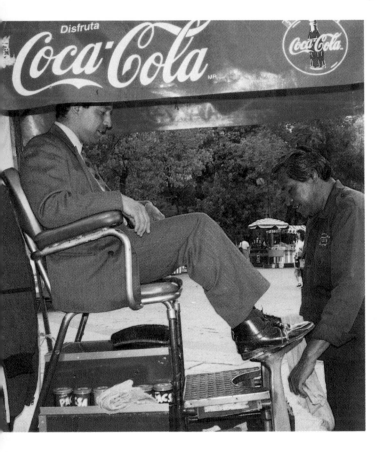

A shoe-shine man tending to a businessman's shoes

polishes the shoes of people who work in the nearby banks and offices. Now, late in the day, he waits for another pair of shoes to shine. How much has he earned so far? Gonzales reaches into his pocket and produces a handful of coins totaling ten pesos—about a dollar and a half in U.S. currency. How is he going to survive? Gonzales has been a shoe-shine man for thirty years and knows the ups and downs of his business. He puts the coins back in his pocket and says, "Sometimes you eat; sometimes you don't."

Studies show that 70 percent of Mexico's people live in poverty, and half of those who are poverty stricken live in dreadful conditions. Most families earn less than U.S. $135 a month.

But there are also families who go out to elegant restaurants and spend $100 on dinner alone. Sometimes the wealthy people make an after-dinner toast. They clink glasses and say, "To Mexico, still the best country in the world to be rich in."

Currency Confusion

For years, Mexican currency traded at 12 ½ pesos to the dollar. It was hailed as the most stable money in Latin America. Then, in 1976, the country devalued the peso to 23 to the dollar. This started an avalanche of new money with diminished value. In the years to come, the peso traded at 3,000 to the dollar. Every few years, government printing presses produced different bills to reflect the peso's collapsing value. In the mid-1990s, the government issued the New Peso (NP), which was simply the old peso with three zeros knocked off. Thus 3,000 old pesos equaled 3 NP. In the stores, old and new pesos were exchanged freely, to everyone's confusion.

To be rich in Mexico means having maids, private cooks, and a driver to pick up the children from school and take them to their soccer games. Paying low wages to these service providers allows the rich to surround themselves with servants. The rich include lawyers, bankers, doctors, and politicians. There are also the super-rich, whose families have owned the best land and the most productive mines for generations. Some reports say that about half the nation's wealth is controlled by two dozen large family groups.

The Minimum Wage, Scant Earnings

Mexico has a minimum-wage law, a rate of pay that employers cannot dip below In the late 1990s, the Mexico City minimum wage was eighteen pesos a day. What will eighteen pesos buy in the Mexican capital? Tacos at a street stand are three to four pesos each. A candy bar is three pesos. A soft drink, if you drink it at the store, is one peso. For a real treat, a worker might go to one of Mexico City's many McDonald's restaurants. There, a Big Mac, large fries, and a malt costs about sixteen pesos—almost an entire day's wages. Most people earn more than the official minimum wage, but masses of workers try to survive on eighteen pesos a day.

In the 1960s and through much of the 1970s, a strong middle class had been developing in Mexico. The middle class was made up of small-business owners, farmers, and schoolteachers. These were educated, hardworking people who looked forward to a bright future. Then in the late 1970s, inflation, caused by the devalued currency, wiped out the savings of middle-class people. Gone were the dreams of sending the children to college, expanding a business, or building a more comfortable house. The majority of middle-class Mexicans never recovered.

Mexico's poor people have little sympathy for the middle class and their declining standard of living. The poor consider the middle class to be wealthy. One such poor person is Irene Beatriz Navarro. She is a thirty-year-old mother of three who works as a maid. "I don't see [the middle class] suffering," she says. "They have nannies. They also have a cook and a washerwoman. I know because I am all those things." In early December, Navarro's boss fired her from her house-cleaning job. She suspects she was dismissed because the boss did not want to pay her a Christmas bonus. "How can I try harder?" Navarro asks. "How? I already try as hard as I can."

The gap between rich and poor and the erosion of the middle class plagues Mexico. Some frustrated poor people escape into lives of drugs and drunkenness. Hopeless poverty was the spark that set off the bloody Mexican Revolution of 1910–1920. Many observers believe another great social upheaval is near. But others point out that Mexico now has a "safety valve." Impoverished workers can cross the border—legally or illegally—and earn a living wage. Some experts believe that without the safety valve of the border, Mexico would explode into a bloody civil war.

The majority of Mexicans live in some degree of poverty.

A Look at the People

In Mexico, Columbus Day—October 12—is a joyful holiday. Many towns have a statue of Columbus somewhere near the town square. On Columbus Day, schoolchildren parade around the statue and decorate it with flowers. Columbus Day is called Día de la Raza (Day of the Race). Columbus is honored because his voyage led to the mestizo people—the mixed European and Indian people who predominate in Mexico today. Interestingly, Columbus never set foot on Mexican soil. It was Hernando Cortés who first brought Spanish blood to the Mexican shores. But Cortés is denounced as a cruel conqueror in most Mexican history books, so there are no statues or holidays to honor him.

A Columbus Day celebration in Guadalajara

THE MESTIZO PEOPLE, CALLED LA RAZA, were born, painfully, out of war and conquest. Four hundred years ago, mestizos were a scant minority in a country of Indians and whites. Today, the vast majority of Mexicans are mestizos. No one knows the exact extent of the mestizo population. Years ago, the government kept census figures dividing the people into three categories: mestizos, Indians, and whites. No such survey has been taken since the 1920s.

Further complicating efforts at racial categorization is the lack of agreement as to who is an Indian. In many respects, being an Indian is a state of mind—a lifestyle. Indians are defined as people who live in a predominantly Indian area and who use Indian phrases in their speech. A mestizo or a white can be considered an Indian under this loose definition.

Opposite: **A mother and child in Chiapas**

Blacks in Mexico

Slavery was permitted during the 300-year era of New Spain. Under Spanish rule, about 200,000 African slaves were taken to Mexico. Long ago, the blacks integrated into the Mexican population. Today, African-Americans from the United States and blacks from other countries claim they get curious stares when visiting remote regions of Mexico because the people are simply not accustomed to seeing black people.

Indians, a Special Way of Life

Mexico's Indian population tends to be concentrated in regions. In certain areas, Indians practice the old ways of life and exist almost as a separate society within Mexico. One such Indian area is the southern state of Chiapas, along the border with Guatemala. The people there, mostly Maya, blend Indian religious customs with Catholicism. Chiapan men and women chant traditional prayers in front of the statues of Catholic saints, but they also leave the saints special gifts. At the foot of the statues, they may place a few eggs or a soft drink. Many hundreds of years ago, the Maya presented gifts to the statues of their gods in much the same manner.

The streets of Mexico City are an ideal place to see the multicolored Mexican people. Mexicans from every part of the country have come to the capital in recent years including blonds, who look like they might very well be natives of Denmark. Maya Indians, whose features are unchanged since before Spanish times, are also found in Mexico City. Mexico is a multiracial society, but one group—the dark-skinned mestizo—is in the majority.

A group of mestizos

Look at situation comedies on Mexican television. The people in the subject family are very often middle-class whites. Then look at the TV advertisements. The woman who claims her favorite brand of detergent performs miracles on her dishes is white. The little boy who praises a gelatin dessert is light-skinned and blond. Ask a Mexican why white people play such a prominent role on TV programs, and you get mixed replies. Many will shrug their shoulders and say, "Well, the advertisers want to sell their products." Meaning, if white people buy the detergent, it must be good.

Mexicans use a special word—*güeros*—to describe white people. Güeros are thought to be handsome, lucky, and rich. There is some truth to equating whiteness with wealth. Hundreds of years ago, white-skinned Spaniards and other Europeans seized Mexico's best farmland and its most productive mines. Whites tended to marry other whites, so for centuries the wealth

Who Lives in Mexico?

Mestizo	60%
Indian	30%
Caucasian	9%
Other	1%

The white people of Mexico are often the wealthiest Mexicans.

remained with light-skinned families. In some ways, the 1910–1920 Revolution was a race war because it pitted rich against poor. Therefore, largely, it was whites against nonwhites.

To this day, white or light-skinned Mexicans are usually wealthier than mestizos or Indians. But more than money is attached to the image of the güero. Whiteness in Mexico is a standard of beauty. This is especially true for a *güera*, a light-skinned woman. A blonde, blue-eyed young woman is coveted by young Mexican men, often regardless of her qualities or her abilities.

Officially, Mexicans praise their Indian past and honor the mestizo race. Yet when a light-skinned baby is born to a mestizo family, everyone rejoices. Ask why they are happy and they'll say, "This baby will prosper because life is so much easier for whites."

Spanish, the National Language

Almost 500 years ago, the Spanish conquerors brought their language to what is now Mexico. Before the conquest, dozens of Indian tongues were spoken in the land. The Spanish lan-

Español Graces the Southwestern United States

It is difficult to describe the spectacular beauty of Texas, New Mexico, and Arizona without using Spanish words—mesa, arroyo, and canyon all have Spanish origins. Such words, originally brought to the region by Mexican pioneers, have become part of southwestern poetry. Colorful cowboy lingo also has Spanish roots. The word *lingo* comes from the Spanish *lengua* (tongue). Other cowboy words such as lariat and corral are also derived from the Spanish. When a cowboy became drunk and disorderly, he ended up in the *calaboose* (jail), a Spanish word meaning dungeon.

guage helped to unify the nation, although many people preferred their old Indian speech. Today, Spanish is the official language of Mexico, and it is the language of the classrooms and the airwaves. Almost all Mexicans speak español.

Some older Mexicans use Indian languages at home, but they speak Spanish on the streets or in the marketplace. Children in such families often grow up believing there is something sinister about Indian languages. Their mothers and fathers speak the old tongue when they do not want the children to follow their conversation. A small percentage of Mexicans in remote areas use Indian languages more frequently than they use Spanish. Prominent Indian languages still spoken include Mayan, Náhuatl—the language of the Aztecs—and Zapotec.

Spanish is the official language of Mexico.

Mexico's Gifts to the Spanish Language

In the Americas, Spaniards were introduced to foods they had never seen before. The words for these new foods went directly from the Indian languages into Spanish. *Jitomate* (hee-to-MAH-teh) for "tomato," and *cacahuate* (cah-cah-WAH-teh) for "peanut" are examples. The word for one animal—coyote—is pronounced nearly the same in Indian, Spanish, and English.

Some Spanish words or phrases are used differently by Mexicans. For example, the Mexican word for matches is *cerillos* (se-REE-os), meaning "wax." In most other Spanish-speaking countries, matches are *fósforos* (fos-FOR-os). To chat informally in Mexico is to *platicar* (plah-ti-CAR), whereas in Spain to chat is *charlar* (char-LAR). Allowing for a few differences in word usage, a Mexican can speak intelligibly with people in any other Spanish-speaking country.

Demographics, the Rush to the Cities

How crowded is Mexico City? Consider a few facts. The Mexico City region is about as big as Rhode Island, but the city and its suburbs hold almost 25 percent of the entire

Mexican population. Greater Mexico City has a larger population than many countries. More people live in the Mexico City area than live in all of Mexico's neighboring countries to the south: Guatemala, El Salvador, Honduras, and Nicaragua. Until recently an accurate census of the city was difficult to take because people were moving in at the rate of 3,000 to 5,000 a day.

The explosive growth of Mexico City and its metropolitan area is a recent development. The city and its suburbs expanded from 1 million in 1930, to 8 million in 1970, to 16 million in 1980, to today's overflowing population of about 22 million. Migration from outlying regions caused this population boom. At one time, people from the country were

More people live in Mexico City than in some entire countries.

The Zocalo

A huge public square called the Zocalo sits in the very center of Mexico City. It is a gathering place where people assemble to hear a patriotic speech by the president or to listen to a rebel politician denounce the government. During Aztec times, these same grounds served as a public square. In Spanish, the word zocalo means "base" or "foundation." For many years, a base for a statue stood there while city leaders argued relentlessly over whose figure should be placed upon it. Finally the base, or zocalo, was removed. No matter. People still called the plaza the Zocalo. Around the country, the public squares of other villages are often called zocalos.

National Polytechnic Institute

Plaza of the Three Cultures

Bosque de Chapultepec

Area of Detail

(Zócalo)

Netzahualcóyotl

Independence Monument

0   2 miles

0   3 kilometers

National Autonomous University of Mexico

Olympic Stadium

← Basilica of Guadalupe (1 mile)

National Art Museum

House of Representatives

City Theater

Senate

Palacio de Belles Artes

Main Temple

Metropolitan Cathedral

Museum of Anthropology (2 miles) →

Zocalo

National Palace

Federal Building

Supreme Court

National Library

Museum of Mexico City

0   0.2 mile

0   0.3 kilometer

Aztec Pyramid

MEXICO CITY CENTER

Mexico City, the World's Biggest Metropolis

Within its official city limits, Mexico City's population is the second-largest in the world. Only Tokyo, Japan, is larger. But Mexico City and its sprawling suburbs, including the city of Netzahualcóyotl, make up the world's biggest metropolitan area. Some 22 million people—almost one of every four Mexicans—live in the Mexico City region. This means that 25 percent of Mexico's population resides on less than 1 per cent of its land area.

Guadalajara, the Second City

"Guadalajara! Guadalajara! You are the soul of the province; you have the lovely smell of an early rose," says a lively song praising Mexico's second-largest city. Like all the nation's cities, Guadalajara has suffered in recent years from overpopulation and air pollution. Still it delights visitors with its fountains, public squares, and tree-shaded parks. The city's restaurants are said to be the best in Mexico. A frothy stew called *pozole* is a favorite Guadalajara dish.

moving to vacant land in the capital so quickly they were called "parachutists" because it seemed they simply dropped out of the sky.

Many thousands of country people settled on a cactus-strewn wasteland that lies on the capital's outskirts. This area has the complicated Aztec name Netzahualcóyotl. Newcomers in Netzahualcóyotl built houses out of scrap bricks, wood, and cardboard. Roofs were fashioned from flattened tin cans hammered together. In just three decades, this collection of huts and shanties grew to become Mexico's third-largest city.

Netzahualcóyotl is a success story of sorts. Mexicans are ingenious in making the best of what little they have. As the suburb grew, the residents built parks and planted trees along the streets. One by one, families tore down their old shacks and replaced them with cinder-block houses. Home owners cleared space to plant gardens and put flowers in window boxes. Netzahualcóyotl no longer has the look of a slum. People living there call it, affectionately, "Netza."

However, the air pollution caused by overcrowding is certainly no success story. The capital and its suburbs are home to 30,000 factories and almost 3 million motor vehicles. Altogether more than 11,000 tons of gaseous wastes pour into the air each day. Because Mexico City is ringed by mountains, there is no way for the pollutants to escape. On windless days, it is difficult to see even across the street. Because of the smog, many Mexico City residents suffer from asthma and chronic eye infections. Many experts claim the capital has the most poisonous air of any city in the world. On particularly bad days, authorities close the schools because the air is considered to be too dangerous for children to venture outside. Short of closing all the factories and prohibiting cars, there seems to be no way to rectify the capital's air-pollution woes. One engineer said that trying to reduce the city's pollution is like trying to "fix an airplane while it's in flight."

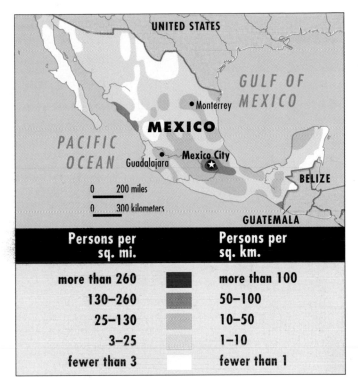

Persons per sq. mi.		Persons per sq. km.
more than 260	■	more than 100
130–260	■	50–100
25–130	■	10–50
3–25	■	1–10
fewer than 3	□	fewer than 1

Mexico's Population Growth

Year	Population
1940	19,654,000
1950	25,791,000
1960	34,923,000
1970	48,225,000
1980	66,847,000
1990	81,140,922
1999 (est.)	105,147,000

Not only the capital but all Mexican cities have experienced runaway growth in the last forty years. Two factors have contributed to the urban explosion. First, Mexico has one of the world's fastest-growing populations. Between 1940 and 1990, the number of Mexicans increased fourfold. Second, the rural economy underwent drastic changes in the 1960s and 1970s. Big farmers bought tractors and other equipment, lessening their need to hire farmhands. Small farmers sold their land to the more efficient large farms. Fewer jobs on the land forced farmworkers to migrate to the cities.

In 1900, about 10 percent of the Mexican population lived in cities and towns; the rest resided in farming areas. Today, almost 80 percent are urban dwellers. Recently, the Mexican birthrate has slowed down. Over the last twenty years, the number of children in a Mexican family has dropped from more than six to an average of 2.5. Also, fewer families are making the mad dash from farms to cities. But Mexico—once a country of farmers—is now solidly an urban society, and the cities are bursting at their seams.

Opposite: **Many Mexicans have become urban dwellers.**

A People of Faith

Look at the people riding on a bus in any city in Mexico. They are chattering away with friends or they are reading newspapers. Then the bus passes a church. Many riders stop what they are doing and silently make the sign of the cross—a hand gesture from forehead to chest, left shoulder to right shoulder. People walking on sidewalks also cross themselves in front of a church. Even some car drivers stop and perform this ritual—and thus create a traffic jam.

ABOUT 90 PERCENT OF THE Mexican people are Roman Catholics although no law declares Catholicism to be a state religion. The Mexican Constitution guarantees freedom of religion to all citizens. Yet the people cling to their church. In recent years, the Mormons, the Episcopalians, and other churches have sent ministers to Mexico in hopes of winning converts. The ministers walk door to door talking to people. Officially they are welcome in the country, but many families have posted signs on their doors that politely but firmly inform the missionaries that they do not wish to talk. The signs say: "This household is Catholic. We do not accept propaganda from other faiths."

Most Mexicans observe Catholic traditions.

Opposite: **The cathedral in Guadalajara**

The Metropolitan Cathedral

Mexico's largest church is the Metropolitan Cathedral, which rises in the heart of Mexico City. A huge Aztec pyramid and temple once stood on the very grounds the cathedral occupies now. The present church was built between 1718 and 1737. An earlier Catholic church was constructed on this spot by Cortés and the Spanish conquerors. Through the years, the Metropolitan Cathedral has been raked by bullets during revolutionary battles and rattled by earthquakes. Still, the ornate church stands proudly and remains the symbol of Mexican Catholicism.

A Good Friday procession

The church and its rituals govern the rhythm of Mexican life. The wild celebration of Carnival begins in February or March, a time of pre-Lenten festivities. At Carnival parties, people dance and stuff themselves with their favorite foods. Then comes Ash Wednesday and the solemn forty-day period of Lent. During Lent, Catholics shun favorite foods and other pleasures. Good Friday in Mexican towns begins with an almost painfully sad procession. Slowly, church members carry religious statues and banners through the streets while spectators watch. Many of the onlookers mouth silent prayers or weep as they ponder Christ's sufferings on the cross. On Easter Sunday, however, the somber mood is lifted. Christ is risen and people hail his glorious resurrection with music, feasting, and laughter.

Religions of Mexico

Roman Catholic	89.7%
Protestant (including Evangelical)	4.9%
Jewish	0.1%
Other	2.1%
None	3.2%

For a brief period during the 1910–1920 Mexican Revolution, the nation's government became—officially, at least—anti-Catholic. The stand against the church was rooted in history. For years, the Catholic Church was the nation's largest landholder. Powerful priests once dictated policies to government officials. Those abuses ended with the 1917 constitution that separated church from government, similar to the lines laid down in United States. However, even in the years when Mexicans rebelled against the church, most people silently kept true to their faith.

The golden-framed portrait of the Virgin of Guadalupe

Guadalupe, the Savior of Mexico

At the beginning of December, highways leading to Mexico City become clogged, not only with cars and trucks as is customary, but with people on foot. Hikers—miles and miles of them—stream toward the capital. They are pilgrims coming to celebrate Guadalupe Day on December 12. On that day, more than 450 years ago, the picture of the Virgin of Guadalupe magically appeared on the straw vest of Juan Diego, an

Indian peasant. The miracle of that event seems to become even more profound with age.

Every year on Guadalupe Day, more than a million people visit the church that holds the picture. For the last mile or so, some pilgrims inch toward the church on their knees, scraping their skin bloody in the process. Some worshipers are dressed in rags. Others wear suits and dresses worth more than the average factory worker earns in a year. The differences between rich and poor, mestizo and Indian melt at the doorway of this special church. As they march to the church, family groups hold signs proclaiming special messages. One sign, held by a woman, says, "My family wishes to thank the Virgin for answering our prayers and curing my baby daughter of a fever."

A new church was built in the 1970s to hold the celebrated painting of the Virgin. Inside the modernistic church, worshipers are whisked past the painting on a moving sidewalk. There is no other way

Sister Juana Inés de la Cruz

Juana Inés de la Cruz was born near Mexico City in 1651. By the age of eight, she was writing poetry, poring over classical literature, and amazing scholars with her knowledge of science. While still a teenager, Juana Inés de la Cruz became a nun. She disturbed powerful priests by writing that the study of science confirms—rather than refutes—the teachings of the Bible. The priests confined her to a cell. According to one legend, she continued writing, using her own blood as ink. During a cholera epidemic, she refused to leave the convent, choosing instead to treat sick nuns. She died of cholera in 1695. Sister Juana Inés de la Cruz was never proclaimed a saint by the Catholic Church. She is instead a religious hero, revered in Mexico for her courage.

to accommodate the masses of people who wish to glimpse the portrait in its golden frame. Experts claim that over the centuries, the straw vest has not deteriorated, nor have the painting's colors faded.

The Day of the Dead

Octavio Paz was Mexico's foremost philosopher and writer and winner of the 1990 Nobel Prize for Literature. He was the first Mexican to win that prestigious award. As a philosopher, he often wrote about the Mexican character. He puzzled over the people's curious mixture of European and American Indian

Holidays in Mexico

New Year's Day	January 1
Carnival	Late February/Early March
Constitution Day	February 5
Flag Day	February 21
Birthday of Benito Juárez	March 21
Easter Week	March or April
International Worker's Day	May 1
Cinco de Mayo (Fifth of May)	May 5
Mother's Day	May 10
Navy Day	June 1
Mexican Independence Day	September 16
Día de la Raza (Columbus Day)	October 12
Día de los Muertos (Day of the Dead)	November 1 and 2
Día de la Revolución (Revolution Day)	November 20
Día de Nuestra Señora de Guadalupe (Guadalupe Day)	December 12
Las Posadas	Begins December 16; ends January 6

influences. In his book *The Labyrinth of Solitude*, Paz discusses the Mexican's unique attitude toward death: "The word death is not pronounced in New York, in Paris, in London, because it burns the lips. The Mexican, in contrast, is familiar with death, jokes about it. . . . True [he fears death], but at least death is not hidden away: he looks at it face to face, with impatience, disdain, or irony."

Octavio Paz, Mexico's foremost author and philosopher

Mexican religious thinking holds that death, like life, is a natural force. This notion is dramatically displayed during the Day of the Dead holiday. Falling on November 2, the Day of the Dead is a combination of All Souls' Day, All Saints' Day, and Halloween. The Halloween aspect is the most obvious. Pictures of playful-looking ghosts appear in store windows. Vendors sell sugary candy shaped like skulls. Skulls are seen everywhere. Children draw a picture of a skull on a shoe box and cut out holes for eyes and a mouth. On the night of November 1, young people burn a candle in the shoe-box skull and go trick-or-treating. Instead of saying "trick-or-treat," though, the Mexican children chant, "Won't you cooperate with the skull?"

On the morning of November 2, family groups have a picnic at the cemetery. The cemetery may seem an odd place for such a family gathering, but not on the Day of the Dead. First, the families gather at the grave of a long-lost grandmother or uncle. They clean the grave, plant some flowers, and say prayers. There is nothing sad about this occasion. It is a time of remembrance and a time to extend companionship to the departed. If the dead person liked a particular song, the family will sing that song. They will also place a banana, a cupcake, or a bottle of soda on the grave as an offering. All graveyard visitors do their part to bring a little cheer to the long lost friend or relative.

Mexicans dot their calendars with countless holidays. There is a Mail Carriers' Day, a day on which everyone offers food and drink to the person delivering the mail on their route. On Teachers' Day, all students are expected to bring candy or flowers to their teacher. So why not hold a holiday for people in the next world? The Day of the Dead is perfectly natural and a very special time of celebration.

Opposite: **A boy lighting candles on the Day of the Dead**

Mexicans at Ease

A strange hush gripped Mexico in July 1994. Few cars were on the streets. Even the newspaper sellers and shoe-shine boys had vanished from the town squares. A foreign visitor might imagine that the people feared a disaster was about to strike. Was a killer hurricane expected? No. Mexico was playing Bulgaria in the World Cup soccer competition. The World Cup takes place once every four years. It is the Olympics of the soccer world.

THE GAME WAS TENSE. THE EERIE SILENCE on the streets was broken by a sudden roar, then an agonizing moan. The people were all watching on television in their homes or in restaurants as the Mexican national team battled Bulgaria. Finally, after three hours, the people rushed outdoors. Some waved Mexican flags. Other sang. Had the Mexican team won? No. They lost to Bulgaria. But the team had reached the semifinals in World Cup competition. On the field, the men played their hearts out. And who knows? The next World Cup games might bring victory. Such is the passion of sports in Mexico.

Mexico playing Bulgaria in World Cup soccer

Soccer, the Ancient Game

Soccer, as we know it, was brought to Mexico by Europeans. But long before Europeans ever arrived on these shores, the peoples of ancient Mexico played a brand of soccer. The game consisted of two teams whose members tried to propel a large rubber ball into an opponent's goal by pushing it with their hips. Competition was grimly serious. In Maya society, the captain of the winning team was allowed to cut off the head of the losing team's captain!

Opposite: **The Ballet Folklórica**

Fútbol (soccer) is easily the country's favorite team sport. High schools and grammar schools have teams and leagues. In remote farm areas, kids play against each other. Such rural games take place on a rocky field where a pair of cacti serve as goal-posts. The devotion to soccer is so great that no one worries over niceties such as proper fields, uniforms, or equipment.

Mexico's second-leading team sport is *béisbol* (baseball). The game was brought to Mexico from the United States in the early 1900s. The language of Mexican baseball is a mixture of English and Spanish.

Governor Avila

One of the first Mexicans to achieve fame in Major League Baseball was Roberto Avila. He was a fleet-footed infielder who played for the Cleveland Indians in the 1950s. Avila grew up playing soccer. When running the bases, he used his soccer skills by deftly kicking the ball out of an opposing player's glove as the opponent tried to tag him out. Avila was well-spoken and college educated. After retiring from baseball, he was elected governor of the state of Veracruz.

A batter is a *bateador*, a pitcher a *pitchador*, and a shortstop is, well, a shortstop. While baseball is a gift from the north, Mexico has repaid the favor by sending many players to the major leagues in the United States and Canada. On Opening Day 1997, eight players in major league line-ups were Mexicans. Mexico's Fernando Valenzuela, who threw a baffling screwball, was an all-star pitcher for the Los Angeles Dodgers for many years.

Basketball is a city game in Mexico. Courts are available in most city parks. Mexico's gentle climate allows outdoor basketball to be played the year round. Grid-iron football, the type played in the United States, enjoys growing popularity. The game is called *fútbol Americano*. The U.S. style of football would draw greater interest if it were not for the equipment the players must wear. Few Mexican schools can afford to buy helmets, shoulder pads, and the other protective gear needed to play the violent game from the north.

Runners and Walkers

Mexican racewalkers have had surprising success in the Olympic Games. Racewalking was unknown in Mexico until 1968. That year a Mexican soldier entered the Olympics and shocked the racewalking world by capturing a bronze medal. Since then, Mexican walkers have won several gold medals in the Olympic Games. Mexico's best distance runners are the Tarahumara Indians of the Copper Canyon. For reasons they cannot explain, the Tarahumara run wherever they go. When hunting a deer they run the animal into exhaustion. Rarely do these great runners enter track meets. The Tarahumara think most organized races—including the 26.2-mile (42-km) marathon—are too short.

Individual sports enjoyed in Mexico include boxing, wrestling, tennis, track and field, and golf. And the greatest of these, according to Mexicans, is boxing.

Boxing, at all levels, excites fans in Mexico. Small villages bring out a ring, erect lights in a farmer's field, and hold an amateur night. In Mexico City, thousands crowd to the Arena Mexico to watch the fights. This love of boxing has reaped rewards. In amateur and professional matches, three peoples win the most gold medals and championships: African-Americans, Cubans, and Mexicans.

Death in the Afternoon

The word *machismo* describes a type of manly—indeed, super-manly—behavior. A "macho" man will not back down from a street fight even if his opponent is a head taller and outweighs him by 50 pounds (23 kg). Critics of Mexican society claim that a majority of Mexican men act in a macho manner. Defenders say this is nonsense and that only a tiny percentage of Mexican males carry on like fools to live up to a macho creed. But no one denies bullfighting is wildly popular in Mexico. The bull-fighter—the *matador*—must stand alone facing a furious animal that weighs up to 1,000 pounds (453 kg). The matador—a hero in Mexico—is making the ultimate macho statement.

Corrida de toros (bullfighting) was brought to Mexico from Spain. Some people denounce it as a blood sport, a senseless display of cruelty to animals. Others hail the corrida for its music, pageantry, and the courage and grace of the matador. The U.S. writer Ernest Hemingway was one such fan of bull-fighting. He wrote a book about the intricacies of bullfighting called *Death in the Afternoon*.

Bullfighting is considered by some to be beautiful.

Bullfights start at about 4 P.M. The bullring in Mexico City, the Plaza Mexico, is the largest such stadium in the world, seating 50,000 people. The spectacle begins with trumpet blasts, band music, and a colorful parade. Leading the parade are the three principal matadors. Usually each of the three matadors fights two bulls, one bull at a time. The matadors wear ornate costumes. Some bullfighters take up to two hours just to get dressed for a contest.

When the field is clear, the first bull is released from a pen. He rushes into the ring stomping, kicking, and full of fury. This is no barnyard bull. These animals are specially bred to fight. A novice bullfighter takes the first charges. The novice must stand, motionless, as the bull rips into his cape. Next comes a *picador,* who is mounted on a horse. The picador spears the bull with a long lance. Then three *banderilleros* rush up to the bull and stick sharply pointed poles into the back of his neck. At this point, the bull is wild with rage and pain. It is time for the matador to make his grand entrance.

Showing no fear, the matador approaches the animal, while fluttering his cape. Again and again, the bull charges as the matador snatches the cape away. At each charge, the bull's pointed horns come perilously close to the matador's body. The crowd shouts *"Olé!"* when the matador makes a particularly daring or graceful move. By exhausting the animal with repeated charges, the matador is controlling it, preparing the bull for the kill. Finally the matador bends over the bull's bowed head with a sword in his hand. He thrusts the sword into the back of the bull's neck, and—Death in the Afternoon!

Is the corrida de toros cruelty or is it high drama? Is courage or brutal machismo on display in the bullring? The debate may never be resolved.

Some see bullfighting as cruel.

History According to Rivera

Diego Rivera's most famous mural is on the wall of the National Palace in Mexico City. The mural shows Rivera's interpretation of Mexican history. On the left side, he depicts Indians living in peace and harmony. Then the Spaniards arrive and enslave the Indians. On the right are scenes of Spanish brutality, including a Spaniard branding an Indian on the face with a hot iron.

The 1910–1920 Revolution left Mexico in a shambles. Fields were barren, whole towns were abandoned, and everyone had lost a close relative to the fighting. Yet star personalities emerged from this wartime destruction. The stars were not generals, politicians, or sports heroes. Instead, the idols of Mexican society were its artists.

The best of Mexico's artistic scene were the muralists. Murals are wall paintings, an ancient Mexican tradition. Hundreds of years ago, the walls of Mayan and Aztec temples were decorated with religious art. After the Mexican Revolution, three muralists—Diego Rivera, José Orozco, and David Siqueiros—won the admiration of the world. They are known today as the Big Three. Their murals and paintings are hailed as masterpieces.

David Siqueiros was as much a political activist as he was a painter. He was in and out of jail for Communist activities. Siqueiros's murals were designed to uplift working men and women. "A muralist must have a theme," he once said. "His mural is his pulpit." One of Siqueiros's murals shows impoverished farmers rising in revolution and seizing a flag from a landowner.

Many of Diego Rivera's murals also had a socialistic slant. Among the Mexican people, the flamboyant Rivera was the most popular of the Big Three muralists. He stood 6 feet (182 cm) tall, sported a scraggly beard, and weighed more than 300 pounds (136 kg). He once described himself as being "attractively ugly." Despite his unkempt appearance, Rivera had a magnetic attraction for women. His wife, Frida Kahlo, her-

Opposite: Madre y Nina by Diego Rivera, an artist known for his portraits as well as his controversial murals

self a celebrated artist, fought furiously with her husband over his many escapades. The Riveras' battles made headlines in the Mexican press. It is remarkable that in Mexico the feuds of two famous artists—rather than squabbles between a couple of movie stars—were popular reading.

A less controversial painter was Rufino Tamayo. He worked primarily on canvas. Tamayo criticized the political nature of the Big Three muralists, claiming they were "engaged in journalism, not art." He learned to appreciate colors by sitting as a child in front of his aunt's fruit stand. The brilliant yellows of the bananas and the rich greens of the limes surrounded the young Tamayo. It is no wonder that Tamayo the painter became a master of color. Tamayo was in his nineties when he died in Mexico City in 1991. Factory workers, waitresses, and taxi drivers wept over his loss. The old man was the father figure of Mexican art, and he was loved by all.

Rufino Tamayo is known for his exceptional use of color in his art.

Music—The Beat of Life

Think of Mexican music, and the driving, toe-tapping beat of the mariachi band comes to mind. Most bands are made up of one vocalist, two violinists, a guitar player, and two horn players. No rule governs this makeup. Throw in a bass violinist and subtract a horn player and you still have a mariachi band. The groups play in nightclubs and private parties, or they wander the streets playing for money. Their music throbs with life. The mariachi band is, like the cactus, a symbol of Mexico.

The mariachi bands usually include violinists, guitarists, and horn players.

The Bellas Artes

At home in Mexico City, the Ballet Folklórico de Mexico performs in a theater building called the Bellas Artes. The theater was built about 100 years ago by President Porfirio Díaz. Constructed of heavy granite blocks, it cost the Mexican treasury millions of pesos. Today it is slowly sinking. Modern Mexico City is built on what was once a lake bed. The granite Bellas Artes is simply too heavy for the soft ground to support. Every year the historic theater sinks a few more millimeters, and no one knows what can be done to stop it from eventually dropping out of sight.

According to legend, mariachi music was born when the French army occupied Mexico in the 1860s. French soldiers married Mexican girls and hired bands to entertain the wedding guests. Mariachi is a mispronunciation of the French word for "marriage." The bands now perform at marriages—and on any other occasion one can imagine. Their music can be sad. Take, for example, the song about the mule driver who lost his girlfriend to another man and now laments, *Mi vida no vale nada* ("My life is worth nothing"). But their very next number will explode with joy, *Allá en el rancho grande, allá donde viviá . . .* ("Out there on the great ranch where I used to live . . .").

Mexicans also enjoy folk music, rock, jazz, classical music, opera, and ballet. Combining folk dancing with lively Latin music, the Ballet Folklórico de Mexico thrills audiences around the world. Members of the ballet wear brilliant costumes and dance with precision as well as passion. The Ballet Folklórico de Mexico is popular everywhere and serves as one of the country's greatest ambassadors.

Visitors to Mexico cannot avoid hearing the people's music, and few would choose to do so. Bands play in restaurants, student groups sing in town squares, and guitarists sit on park benches and strum their tunes. Music is vital to the Mexican soul.

Life in Mexico

For centuries, the village was the cornerstone of Mexican life. It held farm communities together by giving families a central place to shop, socialize, and worship. Most villages were small and sheltered a lifestyle that seemed timeless. By the 1990s, however, many of those villages expanded to become cities. Mexico now has about fifty cities in which more than 100,000 people reside.

R APID EXPANSION HAS altered life in towns and villages. Housing has popped up where cornfields and pasture lands once lay. Sadly, many of the outlying houses are little more than shacks. The makeshift homes were built by families who fled the poverty of farm life for the promise of village jobs. In Mexico, slums are generally found on the outer borders of towns, while rich people's houses stand in the center.

A church is often at the center of a Mexican village.

Many villages have doubled and tripled in population in the last three decades. Traffic jams are now ferocious. Pollution fogs the skies of mountain towns whose air was once pure. Yet two elements resist change in Mexican village life: the town square remains the heart of a community, and the market is its social center.

Most towns were laid out centuries ago in the Spanish style. Streets were designed, like spokes in a wheel, to converge on a square in the center of town. Typically the square

Opposite: **A street in Taxco**

is a tree-shaded plaza. Villagers sit on benches in the tiny park or they walk slowly in the lanes. Squares are graced by statues and bubbling fountains. Mexicans are fiercely proud of their old plazas. They are kept spotlessly clean. The trees are not just trimmed but they are sculpted so that the treetops look like umbrellas.

A plaza in San Miguel de Allende

Cantinflas (1911–1993)

The most popular star for generations of Mexican moviegoers was the comic Cantinflas. As a teenager he tried to become a boxer. His moves in the ring were so funny that the audience—and even his opponent—laughed. From boxing, Cantinflas graduated to films. Movie critics have compared him to the silent screen star Charlie Chaplin. His role was often that of an impoverished but honest working man who survives on his ability to chuckle at his troubles. Charlie Chaplin saw one of Cantinflas's films and declared, "He's the greatest comedian alive!"

Invariably, a church rises at one end of the town square. The church is old and contains a wealth of memories for village families—marriages, communions, holiday masses, and wakes. Opposite the church there might be a government building, which holds a courtroom, the office of the mayor, and perhaps a local jail. The plaza makes up the old downtown section. Nearby are hotels, a movie house, and the city's best restaurants. These days the movie house may be little used since VCRs and cable TV have invaded Mexico. Video rental stores and noisy video game parlors are now common in all the towns.

The town square springs to life at night. After work and after dinner, families come to the square to meet their neighbors and friends. Tiny children dash up and down the lanes playing tag or hide-and-seek. Teenagers flirt. Years ago, flirting was organized in a walk called the *paseo*. "Rules" of the paseo said that girls had to walk clockwise, while boys walked counterclockwise. Now and then they giggled at one another.

Teenagers in the walk called the *paseo*

Near the plaza is the village market. A squat building, holding dozens of stalls, sits at its center. The stalls are about as long as two or three kitchen tables placed end to end. Vendors—usually women—sell fruits and vegetables from these counters. Other stalls in the market building offer poultry, meat, clothes, and hardware items.

So many vendors operate in the typical market that they spill out of the building and sell their goods outside. In some towns the big building is called the "closed market" while the outside section is the "open market." Outdoor vendors spread canvas on the sidewalks and sell pots and pans, audio tapes and CDs, or the latest style of tennis shoes. Many villages designate a particular day of the week as market day and allow more sellers to display their wares. Sunday is the traditional market day throughout the country.

The market is more than a spot to simply buy and sell goods. It is an open-air meeting hall, a place to chat and gossip. Always colorful and always noisy, the market serves as village entertainment. Sellers shout out the prices of their goods and buyers counter with the amount they are willing to pay. Friendly give-and-take haggling over prices is expected in a Mexican market. If a customer is not satisfied at one stand, he or she simply moves on to the next; there are dozens to choose from.

As villages grow and modernize, the old market has competition. Supermarkets, similar to those in the United States and Canada, have appeared on the fringes of towns. They are surrounded by parking lots. Inside, people push carts and take their groceries to checkout lines. No bargaining for prices here. Instead of the traditional haggling, shoppers hear the piped-in melodies of supermarket music. Prices are generally a few pennies cheaper at the modern places, but many people prefer the traditional market and its old ways. They remember years past

Taxco

Taxco is a famous traditional village in the state of Guerrero. The village has a green central plaza fronting a marvelous church. Scores of artists from the United States and Canada live here. Its Spanish colonial architecture is so charming that by law no outside alterations can be made on its historic buildings. Taxco is known as the "Silver City." It lies in the heart of what was once a rich silver-mining district. Today, dozens of highly talented silversmiths work and sell their crafts there.

Many prefer the traditional markets to the modern stores.

when farm families would walk miles to come to town on a Sunday. There the families attended church, shopped at the market, and ended their evening with a stroll in the town square. A comfortable rhythm held sway when the market and the town square were the unrivaled highlights of village life. Many Mexicans still long for the old days.

Work and Leisure

The workday is also changing in Mexico. Not long ago, the vast majority of people either worked on farms or in farm-related village industries. Thus everyone worked close to home. At around noon they came home to enjoy a large midday meal called the *comida*. After comida, while the sun was still high in the sky, families took a short nap, a *siesta*. Then people returned to their jobs and worked until about seven in the evening.

Modern industry now employs the bulk of Mexican workers. Factories demand that people stay at the workplace for eight to ten hours a day. The prolonged comida followed by a siesta is today replaced by a half-hour break for lunch. Industrial Mexico's workday is almost identical to that of the United States and Canada. But Mexicans are slow to forget the simple pleasures of the midday comida. On Sundays, after church, the comida tradition returns to millions of homes.

The Sunday *comida* is important to many Mexican families.

Tex-Mex Cuisine

Common Mexican specialties include frijoles, guacamole, tortillas, tacos, and chili sauce.

Foods from China, Italy, and France are so tasty they have skipped oceans and crossed continents. Mexican food also enjoys this international reputation. Mexican restaurants can be found in nearly every big city in Europe and in Asia. Thousands of Mexican restaurants thrive in the United States. But in the United States, such restaurants tend to serve meals that originated with Mexican people living in Texas. This Tex-Mex cuisine is different from the foods eaten below the border. For example, the U.S. favorite chili con carne (a mixture of chili, beans, and meat) is a Tex-Mex creation, and is unknown in Mexico. Enchiladas served Tex-Mex style are covered with cheese, whereas the same dish in Mexico has little, if any, cheese on top. Tex-Mex food is very tasty, but it is not representative of real Mexican cuisine.

The Sunday comida is the time to invite guests. It is the time for the cook—most often the mother—to display her skills. Perhaps she will prepare chicken covered with mole sauce. Mole is made of a dozen ingredients including crushed nuts, chocolate, and spices. Some mole recipes are so treasured they are handed down in families as a sacred trust. The cook always serves a plate of steaming hot tortillas with the meal. Made of ground corn, the pancake-shaped tortilla is the everyday bread of Mexico. Everyone's favorite—tacos—are simply made with a filling such as cheese or meat rolled in a tortilla.

Enchiladas, often served for Sunday comida, are made by covering stuffed tortillas with a sauce and baking them. For a special Sunday dessert, the family enjoys flan, a rich pudding made from sugar and eggs.

A spicy hot chili sauce accompanies most Mexican meals. The hot sauce has led to the common belief that Mexican foods are fiery to the taste. Not true! Yes, the sauce is hot. It is made of chili peppers that are ground up with a little vinegar and water. A spoonful of chili sauce will set your mouth on fire. But this sauce is served as a side dish. That way, a diner can sprinkle as much—or as little—sauce as desired over the food. While many Mexicans enjoy chili sauce, others shun it. There is nothing basically spicy about Mexican food.

After Sunday the workweek begins anew. Workers go off to their jobs, and children return to school. Bringing education to masses of Mexicans has been a long and painful struggle.

During the Mexican Revolution (1910–1920) only 15 percent of the Mexican people could read and write. Few public schools existed at the time. Wealthy families sent their children to church-run schools that charged tuition. In the years after the revolution, the government made an intense effort to build a modern public school system. But the system did not extend to the nation's isolated rural communities. There, masses of farm children grew up without even seeing a textbook or the inside of a classroom. To this day, many Mexicans older than sixty cannot read or write because they were denied an education in their youth.

The school system in Mexico is now available to all children.

The school system now extends to all children in every corner of Mexico. By law, children must attend school from ages six through fourteen. Students progress through three school levels. *Primaria* (primary school) lasts from grade one through grade six. Next, the student enters *secundaria* (secondary school) for grades seven, eight, and nine. *Preparatoria* (preparatory school) is a three-year program that can be compared to high school in the United States or Canada. After preparatoria, a student with excellent grades can apply for admission to a university.

The modern school system is extensive and costly. More than 10 percent of the national budget is devoted to education. Yet Mexican education is plagued with student dropouts.

About half the students quit school in the secundaria program. This alarming statistic means the children end their education even before they reach the age of fourteen. Meanwhile, the Mexican economy becomes more and more industrialized. The best-paying jobs are in computer science and other high-technology fields. No one who left school at fourteen is likely to qualify for a high-technology job.

Viva la Fiesta

It is a Saturday morning in June in the town of San Miguel de Allende in the state of Guanajuato. A woman walks down the sidewalk lugging a shopping bag. Suddenly a tall man snatches the bag away. He is wearing a black coat, like Count Dracula

Costumed characters on Loco Day

in the movies. The Dracula figure searches through the shopping bag. "What, no bottle of blood? You have no blood for me today?"

Is the woman alarmed? No. She laughs, and so does Dracula. It is Loco Day in San Miguel. This costumed character is the advance party of the Loco Parade that is now winding down the street. *Loco* means "crazy." Members of the parade act and look like lunatics. Led by a brass band, one "loco" wears the white cloak of a doctor and carries a saw as though he is ready and eager to operate on any bystander. A large woman is dressed like a female wrestler and challenges men to a match. No one accepts her offer. Loco Day is a time for everyone to go a little bit wild. In fact, that is the purpose of a Mexican fiesta—forget your cares and go nuts. After all, it's only for a day.

The widely respected philosopher Octavio Paz wrote at length about his fellow Mexicans' devotion to fiestas. Paz was fascinated at how the Mexican personality changes at fiesta time. Take, for example, the farmer who is patiently waiting for rain. Normally, his facial expressions are as unmovable as the Earth itself. Then comes fiesta and the same farmer is dancing and belting out a song. Says Paz, "If we hide within ourselves in our daily lives, we discharge ourselves in the whirlwind of fiesta."

Any party, even a family get-together, is called a fiesta. Grand fiestas are celebrated by a town or by the nation. Family parties are joyful but limited to relatives and close friends. Grand fiestas know no such limits.

Birthdays are acknowledged in Mexico, but a saint's day is greater cause for a family party. Most Mexicans are named

Opposite: **Most towns in Mexico have their own local festivals.**

Las Mañanitas

While the candles on the cake are burning, guests at a saint's day party sing "Las Mañanitas," a kind of "Happy Birthday" song. It has a haunting tune and poetic words:

Estas son las mañanitas	*These are the little mornings*
Que cantaba Rey David	*That King David used to sing about*
Y por el día de su santo	*And for your saint's day*
Que las cantamos aquí.	*We are singing here.*

after saints. Each saint has a feast day once a year. The feast day is also a day of celebration for anyone named after that saint. For example, if you are named after Saint Michael (your name would be Miguel if you are a boy, or Micaela if you are a girl), you celebrate the Feast of Saint Michael on September 29. A saint's day celebration has all the trappings of a typical birthday party in the United States and Canada. Guests bring gifts, candles are lit, and everyone stuffs themselves with cake and sings a special song.

Local fiestas, those celebrated by a town, abound in Mexico. Veracruz is famous for its *Carnival*, the wild party given before the Lenten season. In addition to Loco Day, San Miguel de Allende holds San Miguel (Saint Michael's) Day in late September. In theory, every Mexican named Miguel or Micaela is supposed to come to San Miguel to celebrate a collective Saint Michael's Day bash. Given the crowds and madness that take over the streets, it seems that all the millions of Miguels and Micaelas have indeed crowded into town.

Himno Nacional de México
(National Anthem of Mexico)

Spanish

English Translation

CHORUS

Mexicanos, al grito de guerra
el acero aprestad y el bridón,
y retiemble en sus centros la tierra
al sonoro rugir del cañón.
(repeat previous two lines)

Ciña ¡oh Patria! tus sienes de oliva
de la paz el arcángel divino;
que en el cielo tu eterno destino
por el dedo de Dios se escribió.
Mas si osare un extraño enemigo
profanar con su planta tu suelo
piensa ¡oh Patria querida! que el cielo
un soldado en cada hijo te dio.

CHORUS

¡Patria! ¡Patria! tus hijos te juran
exhalar en tus aras su aliento
si el clarín con su bélico acento
los convoca a lidiar con valor.
¡Para ti las guirnaldas de oliva!
¡Un recuerdo para ellos de gloria!
¡Un laurel para ti de victoria!
¡Un sepulcro para ellos de honor!

CHORUS

CHORUS

Mexicans, at the cry of battle
lend your swords and bridle;
and let the earth tremble at its center
upon the roar of the cannon.
(repeat previous two lines)

Your forehead shall be girded,
oh fatherland, with olive garlands by
the divine archangel of peace,
For in heaven your eternal destiny has
been written by the hand of God.
But should a foreign enemy
Profane your land with his sole,
Think, beloved fatherland, that heaven
gave you a soldier in each son.

CHORUS

Fatherland, fatherland, your children swear
to exhale their breath in your cause,
If the bugle in its belligerent tone should
call upon them to struggle with bravery.
For you the olive garlands!
For them a memory of glory!
For you a laurel of victory!
For them a tomb of honor!

CHORUS

The Famous Mexican Piñata

At a family party—especially a birthday or a saint's day celebration—small children are entertained with the old party game of breaking the piñata. A piñata is a papier-mâché-covered figure of an animal or a bird. At the party, it is hung from a tree. One of the children is then blindfolded and told to hit the piñata with a stick. Candy, toys, and other treats are inside the figure. Other children gather around in a tight ring. As soon as the piñata breaks, everyone dives forward to pick up the goodies inside. Tradition says the smallest child gets the first turn to whack the piñata. When older children take their turns, an adult pulls the piñata up and down with a rope. That way the fun is stretched out to half an hour or more.

Two fiestas celebrated by the entire nation are *Cinco de Mayo* and Independence Day. Cinco de Mayo (Fifth of May) honors the 1862 Battle of Puebla in which a small Mexican force defeated an invading French army. During Cinco de Mayo festivities, military parades are held and politicians make patriotic speeches. Independence Day is also a time for Mexicans to burst with patriotic pride. Independence is heralded with fireworks bursting in the night, bands playing the National Anthem, and people shouting out "Viva Mexico! Viva Mexico!" over and over again.

Guadalupe Day—a day of devotion as well as a day of joy—is held on December 12. The Virgin of Guadalupe means many things to Mexicans. She is the giver of health and hap-

piness. She is also the patron saint of Mexico, the mother of all those who live on the land. The Virgin is the figure around which Mexicans join hands and truly call each other brothers and sisters. Under her banner, they proclaim with one voice: "Viva Mexico! Viva Mexico!"

Fireworks in Mexico City on Independence Day, 1995

Timeline

Mexican History

Corn is cultivated in Mexico.	7000 B.C.
The Olmec civilization thrives on Mexico's Gulf Coast.	1200 – 400 B.C.
A mysterious people build the city of Teotihuacán near present-day Mexico City.	200 B.C.
Maya society reaches great heights.	A.D. 200 – 800
The Toltec civilization rises in the Valley of Mexico.	900
The wandering Aztecs see an eagle perched on a cactus while eating a snake and begin building Tenochtitlán (present-day Mexico City).	1325
Spaniards occupy Cuba.	1511
The Spanish led by Cortés, land in Mexico at present-day Veracruz.	1519
The Spaniards conquer the Aztecs and form New Spain.	1521
The Virgin of Guadalupe makes her appearance to Juan Diego.	1531

World History

2500 B.C.	Egyptians build the Pyramids and Sphinx in Giza.
563 B.C.	Buddha is born in India.
A.D. 313	The Roman emperor Constantine recognizes Christianity.
610	The prophet Muhammad begins preaching a new religion called Islam.
1054	The Eastern (Orthodox) and Western (Roman) Churches break apart.
1066	William the Conqueror defeats the English in the Battle of Hastings.
1095	Pope Urban II proclaims the First Crusade.
1215	King John seals the Magna Carta.
1300s	The Renaissance begins in Italy.
1347	The Black Death sweeps through Europe.
1453	Ottoman Turks capture Constantinople, conquering the Byzantine Empire.
1492	Columbus arrives in North America.
1500s	The Reformation leads to the birth of Protestantism.

Mexican History		World History	
		1776	The Declaration of Independence is signed.
		1789	The French Revolution begins.
Father Hidalgo inspires the Mexican War of Independence.	1810		
War of Independence is concluded; Mexico is an independent nation.	1821		
Mexico fights a war with the United States; hands over territories to the United States.	1846–1848		
The French army occupies Mexico and installs Maximilian of Austria as emperor; Maximilian is executed by forces loyal to President Benito Juárez.	1863–1867	1865	The American Civil War ends.
Porfirio Díaz becomes president.	1876		
Revolutionary War rages in Mexico.	1910		
		1914	World War I breaks out.
		1917	The Bolshevik Revolution brings Communism to Russia.
		1929	Worldwide economic depression begins.
Mexico participates in the Bracero Program	1942–1945	1939	World War II begins, following the German invasion of Poland.
		1957	The Vietnam War starts.
Mexico devalues its currency from 12.5 pesos to the U.S. dollar to 23 pesos to the dollar.	1976		
A devastating earthquake strikes Mexico City.	1985		
Cuauhtémoc Cárdenas narrowly loses the presidential election; Carlos Salinas de Gortari is elected president.	1988	1989	The Berlin Wall is torn down as Communism crumbles in Eastern Europe.
Luis Donaldo Colosio, a leading presidential candidate, is shot and killed while campaigning in Tijuana.	1993		
The North American Free Trade Agreement (NAFTA) goes into effect. Ernesto Zedillo Ponce de Léon is elected president.	1994		
		1996	Bill Clinton re-elected U.S. president.

Fast Facts

Official name: *Estados Unidos Mexicanos* (United Mexican States)

Capital: Mexico City

Mexico City

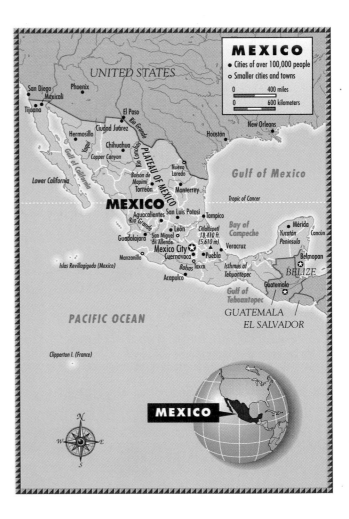

A mariachi band

Flag of Mexico

Bullfighting

Official language:	Spanish
Official religion:	None
National Anthem:	*"Himno Nacional de México"* (National Anthem of Mexico)
Government:	Federal republic with two legislative houses (Senate and Chamber of Deputies)
Chief of state and head of government:	President
Area:	756,066 square miles (1,958,201 sq km)
Coordinates of geographic center:	23° 00' N, 102° 00' W
Bordering countries:	To the west and south is the Pacific Ocean and to the east, the Caribbean Sea and the Gulf of Mexico. To the north is the United States and to the southeast are Guatemala and Belize.
Highest elevation:	Citlalépetl (also called Orizaba), 18,410 feet (5,610 m)
Lowest elevation:	Mexicali Valley, 33 feet (10 m) below sea level
Average temperatures:	in the *tierra caliente* (hot land), 77°F (25°C) in the *tierra templada* (temperate land), 66°F (19°C) in the *tierra fría* (cold land), 63°F (17°C)

Average annual rainfall:

North-northwest	less than 10 inches (25 cm)
Coastal plains	40 to 115 inches (100 to 290 cm)
Chiapas highlands	more than 200 inches (500 cm)

National population (1996 est.):	92,711,000

The Zocala

The Metropolitan Cathedral

New Pesos

Population of largest cities in Mexico (1990):		
	Mexico City	9,815,795
	Guadalajara	1,650,042
	Netzahualcóyotl	1,255,456
	Monterrey	1,068,996
	Puebla	1,007,170

Famous landmarks:
▶ *Bellas Artes* (Mexico City)

▶ *Canon del Rio Blanco National Park* (Veracruz)

▶ *Chichén Itzá* (Yucatán)

▶ *Copper Canyon* (south of Chihuahua)

▶ *Cuernavaca* (resort south of Mexico City)

▶ *Metropolitan Cathedral* (Mexico City)

▶ *Taxco* (village in Guerrero)

▶ *Teotihuacán,* home to the Pyramid of the Sun and the Pyramid of the Moon (near Mexico City)

Industry: Mexican factories produce concrete, iron and steel, clothing, and electronics. Oil production is second only to manufacturing, while tourism is a major source of employment. Mining includes silver, copper, gold, lead, salt, and zinc.

Currency: Peso (equals 100 centavos)

New Peso: NP 8.46 = US$1 (February 1998)

Weights and measures: Metric system

Literacy: 86%

Yucatán Peninsula

Benito Juárez

Pancho Villa

Common Mexican words and phrases:

bueno	good
¿Cómo est usted?	How are you?
gracias	thank you
por favor	please
¿Qué hora es?	What time is it?

Famous Mexicans:

Carlos Chávez Conductor and composer	(1899–1978)
Porfirio Díaz Soldier and politician	(1830–1915)
Miguel Hidalgo y Costilla Priest and revolutionary	(1753–1811)
Juana Inés de la Cruz Poet and scholar	(1651–1695)
Benito Juárez President	(1806–1872)
Frida Kahlo Artist	(1907 1954)
José Clemente Orozco Painter	(1883–1949)
Octavio Paz Writer, Nobel Prize winner	(1914 1998)
Lopéz Portillo, José President	(1920–)
Diego Rivera Painter	(1886–1957)
Rufino Tamayo Artist	(1899–1991)
Francisco "Pancho" Villa Revolutionary	(c.1877–1923)
Emiliano Zapata Revolutionary	(c.1879–1919)
Ernesto Zedillo Ponce de Léon President	(1951–)

To Find Out More

Nonfiction

▶ Casagrande, Louis, and Sylvia Johnson. *Focus on Mexico: Modern Life in an Ancient Land*. Minneapolis: Lerner, 1989.

▶ Greene, Jacqueline D. *The Maya*. New York: Franklin Watts, 1992.

▶ Hoyt-Goldsmith, Diane. *Day of the Dead: A Mexican American Celebration*. New York: Holiday House, 1994.

▶ Irizarry, Carmen. *Passport to Mexico*. New York: Franklin Watts, 1994.

▶ Kent, Deborah. *Mexico*. New York: Marshall Cavendish, 1996.

▶ Larsen, Anita. *Montezuma's Missing Treasure*. Parsipanny, N.J.: Silver Burdette, 1992.

▶ Macdonald, Fiona. *How Would You Survive as an Aztec?* New York: Franklin Watts, 1995.

▶ Morrison, Marion. *Places and People: Mexico and Central America*. New York: Franklin Watts, 1995.

▶ Ochoa, George. *The Fall of Mexico City*. Parsippany, N.J.: Silver Burdette, 1989.

▶ Stein, R. Conrad. *The Aztec Empire*. New York: Marshall Cavendish, 1996.

▶ Stein, R. Conrad. *The Mexican Revolution: 1910–1920*. New York: Macmillan, 1994.

▶ Walsh Shepherd, Donna. *The Aztecs*. New York: Franklin Watts, 1992.

Biography

▶ Bains, Rae. *Benito Juarez, Hero of Modern Mexico*. Mahwah, N. J.: Troll, 1992.

▶ Jacobs, William Jay. *Coronado: Dreamer in Golden Armor.* New York: Franklin Watts, 1994.

▶ Jacobs, William Jay. *Cortés: Conqueror of Mexico.* New York: Franklin Watts, 1994.

▶ Roman, Joseph. *Octavio Paz, Mexican Poet and Critic.* New York: Chelsea House, 1994.

▶ Venezia, Mike. *Diego Rivera.* Chicago: Childrens Press, 1994.

Fiction

▶ Srasser, Todd. *The Diving Bell.* New York: Scholastic, 1994.

Folktales

▶ Aardema, Verna, and Petra Mathers (illustrator). *Borreguita and the Coyote: A Tale from Ayutla, Mexico.* New York: Knopf, 1991.

▶ Madrigal, Antonio Hernandez, and Tomie De Paola (illustrator). *The Eagle and the Rainbow: Timeless Tales from Mexico.* Golden, Colo.: Fulcrum Publishers, 1997.

▶ Rohmer, Harriet, and Mary Anchondo (illustrator). *How We Came to the Fifth World: A Creation Story from Ancient Mexico.* San Francisco: Children's Book Press, 1988.

Websites

▶ **Arts and History: Virtual Forum of Mexican Culture**
http://www.arts-history.mx/direc2.html
A vast website filled with pages of art, history, museums, and other cultural items

▶ **Consulate General of Mexico in New York**
http://www.quicklink.com/mexico/ingles/ing.htm
Extensive information on the Mexican government, cultural organizations, and economy. Provides many links to other pages.

▶ **World Factbook Page on Mexico**
http://www.odci.gov/cia/publications/factbook/country-frame.html
An excellent overview of the geography, government, and economy of Mexico

Organizations and Embassies

▶ **Embassy of Mexico**
1911 Pennsylvania Avenue, N.W.
Washington, DC 20006
(202) 728-1600

▶ **Mexican Government Tourism Office**
405 Park Avenue, Suite 1401
New York, NY 10022
(212) 755-7261

Index

Page numbers in *italics* indicate illustrations

A

African people
    Olmec people and, 31
    slavery and, 73
agriculture, 30, 33, 64–65, 67
    map, 66
    Olmec people, 31
    Tláloc (Aztec rain god), 19
air pollution, 55, 83
Alamo, 39, *39*
animal life, 26
    birds, 29
    Copper Canyon, 26
    effect of highways on, 24
    iguanas, 29, *29*
    jaguars, 25, *25*
    mammoths, 30
    ocelots, 29
    Sierra Madre mountain ranges, 24–25
    spider monkeys, 29
    vultures, 27, *27*
archaeological map, 39
art, 43, 104
    David Siqueiros, 104
    Diego Rivera, 104, 106, 133
    Frida Kahlo, 104, 106, 133
    José Orozco, 104, 133
    murals, 104
    Rufino Tamayo, 106, *106*, 133
Ash Wednesday, 89
Atlantic Ocean, 16
Avila, Roberto, 98, *98*
Aztec people, 32–33
    European disease and, 35
    Montezuma (emperor), 34
    murals, 104
    religion of, 32–33, *33*
    Templo Mayor (Main Temple), 36, *36*
    Tenochtitlán, 32, *32*, 34–35, *35*, 48
    war with Spain, 34–35

B

Ballet Folklórico de Mexico, 96, 108–109
baseball. *See* béisbol.
Basilica of Guadalupe, 11, *12*
basketball, 99
beach resorts, 19
béisbol (baseball), 98–99
    Roberto Avila, 98, *98*
Bellas Artes, 108, *108*
border crossings, 61, *61*
borders, 55–56, *57*, 60. *See also* illegal
    immigration.
    drug–smuggling, 56
    territorial disputes, 38
boxing, 100
    Julio César Chávez, 100, *100*
Bracero program, 43–44, *44*
bullfighting. *See* corrida de toros.

C

cactus, 27, *27*
Cantinflas, 113, *113*
Cárdenas, Cuauhtémoc, 50
Cárdenas, Lazaro, president of Mexico, 54
Catholicism, 87, *87*
census, 73
Chamber of Deputies, 51
Chávez, Julio César, 100, *100*
Chiapas, 74
chiclets (gum), 28
chili sauce, 119
churches, 111, *111*, 113
Cinco de Mayo, 126

cities. *See also* villages.
    Dolores Hidalgo, 38
    Guadalajara, 82
    Guanajuato, 37, *37*
    Mexico City, 78–81, *80*, *81*
    Monterrey, 58, *58*, 60
    Netzahualcóyotl, 82
    Spanish colonial architecture in, 37
    Tenochtitlán, 32, *32*, 34–35, *35*, 48
    Teotihuacán, 31
climate, 18–19, *18*
    Plateau of Mexico, 18
    rainy season, 19
    tierra caliente (hot land), 19
coastline, 16, *17*. *See also* tourism.
Colosio, Luis Donaldo, 53, *54*
Columbus, Christopher, 72
Columbus Day, 72, *73*
comida (midday meal), 116–117, *117*, 119
Constitution of 1917, 43, 49
    freedom of religion, 87
    separation of church and state, 90
Copper Canyon, 25, *25*
    animal life in, 26
    Tarahumara Indians, 26
corrida de toros (bullfighting), 102–103, *103*
Cortés, Hernando, 14, 34, *34*, 72
currency, 69
    minimum-wage law, 69

D

dance
    Ballet Folklórico de Mexico, 96, 108–109
Day of the Dead, 93–95, *94*
Death in the Afternoon (Ernest Hemingway), 101
Democratic Revolutionary Party. *See* PRD (Democratic Revolutionary Party).
Día de la Raza (Day of the Race), 72
Díaz, Porfirio, president of Mexico, 40–41, 108, 133
Diego, Juan, 9, 11, *13*, 90–91
Dolores Hidalgo, 38
drug-smuggling, 56

E

earthquakes, 20–21, 23
    Pacific Ring of Fire map, *23*
Easter, 89
economy, 58, 60–61, 68, *68*, 71
    agriculture, 19, 30–31, 33, *64–65*, 67
    currency, 69
    inflation, 44
    manufacturing, 58, *63*, *64–65*, 67
    middle class, 70
    minimum-wage law, 69
    mining, 37, 67
    NAFTA (North American Free Trade Agreement), 62
    oil industry, 67
    open-air businesses, 18
    outdoor markets, 114
    poverty, 68, 70, *70*, *71*
    service industries, 66
    tourism, 16, *17*, 19, 66
    upper class, 69
education, 44, 120, *120*, 121
    preparatoria (preparatory school), 120, 121
    primaria (primary school), 120
    secundaria (secondary school), 120
Election Day, 47, *47*
elections, 47–48, 50–51
employment, 58–61. *See also* NAFTA (North American Free Trade Agreement).
enchiladas, 119
Estados Unidos Mexicanos (United Mexican States), 46
executive department (of government), 49

F

Famous people
    Benito Juárez, 41, *41*, 133, *133*
    Carlos Chávez, 100, *100*, 133
    Diego Rivera, 104, 106, 133
    Emiliano Zapata, 41, 43, *43*, 133
    Ernesto Zedillo Ponce de Leon, 133
    Francisco "Pancho" Villa, 41, *42*, 133
    Frida Kahlo, 104, 106, 133
    José Clemente Orozco, 104, 133
    Juana Inés de la Cruz, 91, *91*, 133

Lopéz Portillo, 133
Miguel Hidalgo y Costilla, 38, *38*, 133
Octavio Paz, 92–93, *93*, 124, 133
Porfirio Díaz, 40–41, 108, 133
Rufino Tamayo, 106, *106*, 133
Feast of Saint Michael, 126
federal district, 46
fiesta, 121–127, *122*
flag, 48, *48*
flan (pudding), 119
foods, 118, *118*
    chiclets (gum), 28
    chili sauce, 119
    comida (midday meal), 116–117, *117*,
      119
    enchiladas, 119
    flan (pudding), 119
    mangoes, 28, *28*
    mole sauce, 119
    nopal (cactus), 27–28
    papaya fruit, 28
    pozole, 82
    tacos, 119
    Tex-Mex cuisine, 118
    tortillas, 119
    tuna (cactus fruit), 28
football. *See* fútbol Americano.
French occupation of Mexico, 40
fútbol (soccer), 97–98
    World Cup competition, 96–97, *97*
fútbol Americano (grid-iron football),
    99

G

geography, 14–17
    earthquakes, 20–21, 23
    map, *15*
    volcanoes, 22, *22*
geopolitical map, *10*
gold mines, 37
Good Friday, 89, *89*
government, 47, *55*
    Chamber of Deputies, 51
    Constitution of 1917, 43, 49, 87, 90
    executive department, 49
    federal district, 46
    judicial department, 49

legislative department, 49
licenciado (legal aide), 51
mordida (little bite), 51, 53, 52
New Spain, 37–38
presidente (president), 47, 49
states, 46
Guadalajara, *73*, 82, 86
Guadalupe Day, 127
Guanajuato, 37, *37*
güeros/güeras (white people), 75–76, *75*
Gulf of Mexico, 16

H

Hemingway, Ernest
    Death in the Afternoon, 101
Hidalgo y Costilla, Miguel, 38, *38*, 133
holidays
    Ash Wednesday, 89
    Cinco de Mayo, 126
    Columbus Day, 72
    Day of the Dead, 93–95, *94*
    Easter, 89
    Feast of Saint Michael, 126
    Guadalupe Day, 90, 127
    Independence Day, 126, *127*
    Lent, 89
    Loco Day, *123*, 123–124
    Mail Carriers Day, 95
    Teachers Day, 95
Huerta, Victoriano, president of Mexico,
    42

I

iguanas, 29, *29*
illegal immigration, 61–62. *See also* borders.
Independence Day, 126, *127*
Inés de la Cruz, Juana, 91, *91*, 133
inflation, 44

J

jaguars, 24, *25*
Juárez, Benito, president of Mexico, 41,
    41, 133, *133*
Judicial department (of government), 49

K

Kahlo, Frida, 104, 106, 133

L

La Raza. *See* mestizo people.
Labrynth of Solitude, The (Octavio Paz), 93
language, 76–77, *77*
    pronunciation, 78
Las Mañanitas (saint's day party song), 124
legislative department (of government),
    47, 49
Lent, 89
licenciado (legal aide), 51
literature
    Octavio Paz, 92–93, *93*, 124, 133
Loco Day, *123*, 123–124

M

Madre y Nino (Diego Rivera), *105*
Mail Carriers Day, 95
mammoths, 30
mangoes, 28, *28*
manufacturing, 58, *63*, 67
    maquiladores (factories), 64–65
maps
    agricultural, 66
    archaeological, *39*
    geographical, *15*
    geopolitical, *10*
    Mexican City Center, *81*
    Mexican Revolution, *44*
    Pacific Ring of Fire, *23*
    population, *83*
    province, *47*
    resource, *66*
    territorial losses, *40*
maquiladores (factories), 64–65
mariachi bands, *107*, 109
Maximilian (archduke of Austria), 40
Maya people, 26, *26*, 31–32, 74
    Mayan ruins, *30*
    murals, 104
mestizo people, 36, 72–74, *74*
Metropolitan Cathedral, 88, *88*
Mexican Revolution, 42–43, 71
    map, *44*
Mexican-American War, 39–40
    Alamo, 39, *39*
Mexico City, *21*, 79, 81, *81*
    City Center map, 81

earthquakes in, 21–23, *23*
    as largest metropolitan area, 81
    Metropolitan Cathedral, 88, *88*
    National Palace, 46
    population of, 78–79, 82
    Zocalo (public square), 80, *80*
middle class, 70
minimum-wage law, 69
mining, 67
    gold, 37
    silver, 37, 67
mole sauce, 119
Monterrey, 58, *58*
    employment in, 60
Montezuma (Aztec emperor), 34, *34*
mordidas (little bite), 51, 53, *52*
mountain lions, 24
mountains
    animal life in, *15*, 24, 26–27
    Sierra Madre ranges, 15–16, 24–25
murals, 104
Museum of Anthropology, 20, *20*
music, 107
    Las Mañanitas (saint's day party song),
        124
    mariachi bands, 107, *107*, 109
    national anthem, 125

N

NAFTA (North American Free Trade
    Agreement), 62–64. *See also* employ-
    ment.
National Action Party. *See* PAN
    (National Action Party).
national anthem, 125
National Palace, 46
Netzahualcóyotl, 82
New Spain, 35
    government of, 37
nopal (cactus), 27–28
North American Free Trade Agreement.
    See NAFTA (North American Free
    Trade Agreement).

O

ocelots, 29
oil industry, 67

Olmec people, 31
    African people and, 31
    monuments, 31, *31*
Olympic Games, 99
Open-air businesses, 18, 114–115, *116*
Orozco, José, 104, 133
Our Lady of Guadalupe, 9

P

Pacific coast, 16
Pacific Ring of Fire map, *23*
PAN (National Action Party), 51
papaya fruit, 28
Party of Revolutionary Institutions. *See* PRI
    (Party of Revolutionary Institutions).
paseo (flirting walk), 113, *114*
Paz, Octavio, 92–93, *93*, 124, 133
    Labyrinth of Solitude, The, 93
people, 85. *See also* Famous people.
    African, 31
    Aztec, 32–33
    güeros/güeras (white people), 75–76, *75*
    Indian, 74
    Maya, 26, *26*, 31–32, 74
    mestizo, 36, 74, *74*
    Mexican Americans, 56
    population, 59
    racial categorization, 73
    Tarahumara Indians, 26
    teenagers, 51, 113, *114*
peso (currency), 69
piñata, 126, *126*
plant life, 26
    cactus, 27, *27*
    flowers, 28
    mangoes, 28, *28*
    nopal (cactus), 27–28
    papaya fruit, 28
    saguaro (giant cactus), 27
    sapodilla tree, 28
    tuna (cactus fruit), 28
Plateau of Mexico, 16
    climate, 18
plazas, 111–113, *112*
population, 59
    census, 73
    growth rate, 84
    map, *83*

Mexico City, 78–79, 82
poverty, 68, 70, *70*, 71
pozole (food), 82
PRD (Democratic Revolutionary Party), 50
    Cuauhtémoc Cárdenas and, 50
preparatoria (preparatory school), 120, 122
presidente (president), 47
    elections, 49
PRI (Party of Revolutionary Institutions),
    48
    Carlos Salinas de Gortari, president of
        Mexico and, *49*, 50
    Luis Donaldo Colosio, *53*, 54
primaria (primary school), 120
province map, *47*
Pyramid of the Moon, 31
Pyramid of the Sun, 31, *31*

Q

Quetzalcóatl (Aztec god), 34

R

racewalking, 99
racial categorization, 73
religion, 86
    Ash Wednesday, 89
    Aztec, 32–33, *33*
    Catholicism, 87, *87*
    churches, *111*, 113
    Easter, 89
    Good Friday, 89, *89*
    Juana Inés de la Cruz, 91, *91*, 133
    Lent, 89
    Maximilian (archduke of Austria), 40
    Metropolitan Cathedral, 88, *88*
    Quetzalcóatl (Aztec god), 34
    Spain and, 34
    Virgin of Guadalupe, 92
resource map, 66
Rio Grande
    as border, 55
    illegal immigration and, *61*, 62
Rivera, Diego, 104, 106, 133
    Madre y Nino, *105*

S

saguaro (giant cactus), 27
Salinas de Gortari, Carlos, president of

Mexico, *49, 50,* 54
San Miguel de Allende, *112*
sapodilla tree, 28
secundaria (secondary school), 120
service industries, 66
Sierra Madre mountain ranges, 15–16
    animal life in, 24–25
silver mining, 37, 67
Siqueiros, David, 104
slavery, 73
soccer. *See* fútbol.
Spain
    colonial architecture, 37
    European disease and, 35, 37
    invasion by, 34–37
    slavery and, 73
    war with Aztec people, 34
spider monkeys, 29
sports
    basketball, 99
    béisbol (baseball), 98–99
    boxing, 100
    Chávez, Julio César, 100, *100,* 133
    corrida de toros (bullfighting),
        101–103, *101, 103*
    fútbol (soccer), 98
    fútbol Americano (grid-iron football),
        99
    Julio César Chávez, 100, *100*
    Olympic Games, 99
    racewalking, 99
    World Cup competition, 96–97, *97*
states
    governors, 47
    legislature, 47
street vendors, 18, 59, *59*

T
tacos, 119
Tamayo, Rufino, 106, *106,* 133
Tarahumara Indians, 26
Taxco, *110, 115*
Teachers Day, 95
teenagers, 51
    paseo (flirting walk), 113, *114*
Templo Mayor (Main Temple), 36, *36*
Tenochtitlán, 32, *32,* 34, 48
    destruction of, 35, *35*

Teotihuacán, 31
territorial losses map, *40*
Tex-Mex cuisine, 118
tierra caliente (hot land), 19
tilma (straw vest), 11
Tláloc (Aztec rain god), 19–20
tortillas, 119
tourism, 16, *17,* 66
    beach resorts, 19
tuna (cactus fruit), 28

U
United Mexican States. *See* Estados
    Unidos Mexicanos.
United States
    border with, 55–56, *57,* 60
    as El Norte (The North), 55
    illegal immigration to, 61–62
    Spanish influence on language of, 76
    territorial disputes with, 38
upper class, 68, 69

V
Villa, Francisco "Pancho", 41, *42,* 133
villages, 110–111. *See also* cities.
    churches in, 111
    outdoor markets, 114–115, *116*
    plazas, 111–113, *112*
    San Miguel de Allende, 112
    Taxco, *110, 115*
Virgin of Guadalupe, 11–13, *13,* 90, 91–92
    Guadalupe Day, 90, 127
volcanoes, 22, *22*
vultures, 27, *27*

W-Z
War of Independence, 38
World Cup competition, 96–97, *97*
World War II, 43

Yucatán Peninsula, 17
    bird life, 29

Zapata, Emiliano, president of Mexico,
    41, 43, *43,* 133
Zapatistas (rebels), 45, *45*
Zocalo (public square), 80, *80*
Zumárraga (bishop of Mexico City),
    9, 11–12

Meet the Author

R. CONRAD STEIN was born and grew up in Chicago. He served in the U.S. Marines and later earned a degree in history from the University of Illinois. He then studied at and received an advanced degree from the University of Guanajuato in Mexico. The author has published more than eighty books for young readers. He now lives in Chicago with his wife and their daughter Janna.

Mr. Stein lived in Mexico through most of the 1970s. The author and his family return to the Mexican town of San Miguel de Allende, their second home, each summer. Over the years, Mr. Stein has seen vast changes in Mexico, but he still loves the country. At fiestas he proudly joins crowds on the streets and shouts out, "Viva Mexico! Viva Mexico!"

Photo Credits

Photographs ©:

All-Sport USA: 97 (Dave Leah), 100 (Holly Stein);
AP/Wide World Photos: 127 (Carlos Taboada), 44, 98, 113;
Archive Photos: 42, 133 bottom; BBC **Natural History Unit:** 25 bottom (Gerry Ellis), 27 (Jurgen Freund);
Bridgeman Art Library International Ltd., London/New York: 91 (Sister Juana, Grand daughter of D. de Cortes, Founder of Convent of St. Jerome, c.1661 Museo de America, Madrid);
Comstock: 36, 116 (Stuart Cohen), 7 bottom, 29, 69, 73, 96, 132 bottom; e.t. archive: 34 bottom;
Gamma-Liaison: 9, (George Swain), 20 (Arvind Garg), 30 (George Swain), 45 (Alyx Kellington), 47 (Dante Busquets-Sordo), 49 (Stephen Ferry), 50 (Dryden), 63 (Burroughs), 70, 71 (Paul S. Howell), 72 (Dante Busquets-Sordo), 80 (Aaron Strong), 93 (Swersey), 101 (Bill Sallaz), 103 (John Annerino), 122 (Lyle Leduc), 131 bottom (John Annerino), 132 top (Aaron Strong);
Impact Visuals: 74, 79 (Jana Birchum);
International Stock Photo: 14 (J. Contreras Chacel), 15 (Buddy Mays), 19 (Hollenbeck), 21 (J. Contreras Chacel), 31 bottom, 37 (Cliff Hollenbeck), 94 (George Ancona), 107, 121, 131 top (Cliff Hollenbeck);

Masako Takahashi: 12, 13, 16, 52, 68, 87, 88, 112, 114, 117, 120, 123, 132 center;
National Geographic Image Collection: 60, 61 (Joel Sartore);
Nik Wheeler: 2, 7 top, 18, 23, 24, 25 top, 28, 59, 81, 108, 110, 111, 130;
North Wind Picture Archives: 32 bottom, 33, 35, 39, 41, 43, 133 center;
Panos Pictures: 17 (David Constantine), 31 top, 118 (Ron Giling), 133 top (David Constantine);
PNI: spine (Jean Colin/Wood River Gallery)
Reuters/Archive Photos: 53 (Silvia Calatayud);
Robert Fried: 77, 82, 86; Superstock, Inc.: 8 (Christie's Images/SuperStock), 32 top (Anthropological Museum, Mexico/ET Archive, London/SuperStock), 34 top (Newberry Library, Chicago/SuperStock), 105 (Christie's Images), 115, 38;
The Image Works: 22 (F. Rangel), 26, 46 (Macduff Everton), 57 (Bob Strong), 58 (L. Mangino), 64, 65, 75 (Macduff Everton), 85 (David Wells), 89, 90 (F. Rangell), 106 (Algaze);
Tony Stone Images: cover, 6 (Bob Torrez), 48, 131 center (Ken Biggs).

Maps by Joe LeMonnier